DATE DUE

☆ THE CONSERVATIVE AMERICAN ☆

Books by Clarence Manion

LESSONS IN LIBERTY

THE KEY TO PEACE

LET'S FACE IT

MEN OF PRINCIPLE

THE CONSERVATIVE AMERICAN

THE
CONSERVATIVE
AMERICAN

☆☆☆☆☆

*His Fight for National Independence
and Constitutional Government*

by CLARENCE MANION

THE DEVIN-ADAIR CO., New York

1964

FOR
Gina
Marilyn
Carolyn
Dan
Diana and
Chris—
Bright tomorrows in a Free America

☆ ACKNOWLEDGMENTS ☆

With this publication, immeasurable gratitude goes to hundreds of American patriots, living and dead, whose enduring principles, firm purposes and inspiring expressions have enriched the recollections of this author. In a very real sense, much of this book is but a codification of what these dedicated people have been writing and saying to each other and to me for more than a quarter of a century. Credit lines for all of those who deserve them would be impossible.

I am particularly grateful for the professional assistance of my legal associate, Mrs. Lora D. Lashbrook, in the preparation of the manuscript and its documentation.

Foreword

The Conservative American is afflicted with principle. The political "art of the possible" leaves him cold. A prolonged diet restricted to choices between acknowledged evils has given him a bad case of political ulcers. He is allergic to expedient compromises and he would rather be defeated in a righteous cause than win by the sanctification of sophistries.

The Conservative American lacks capacity for "practical politics." Career politicians—the case-hardened, heat-tempered "Old Pro's"—hate to see him coming. In the black art of politics, organizational regularity demands that after the party's candidates have been named, loyal partisans shall "rise above principle" and dutifully support the entire ticket in the general election. The Conservative American shatters this article of political faith by threatening to "take a walk" on election day if his principles are not embraced by the party's nominees.

In political thought and action the Conservative American has been an individualist. Through the years he has become accustomed to the isolation of non-conformity and if he has not learned to like it, he has at least become reconciled to the comparative solitude of the sidelines. But Conservative Americanism has suddenly become gregarious. Its cumulus clusters on the "right" of the political front have recently been heard to thunder. The established political order is definitely concerned. What casts this lengthening shadow? A man perhaps, or is it a movement? What are the ultimate dimensions of this big rumble on the right? Who is this Conservative American? What wound him up? What makes him tick and where does he think he is going? Nobody has all the answers, but some of them are printed in this book. Others will be found between the lines. Somewhere after the beginning and before the end a composite photograph will be developed. It may turn out to be a picture of you.

C. M.

South Bend, Indiana

Contents

✩ ✩ ✩ ✩ ✩

Contents

PART ONE

☆ THE CONSERVATIVE AMERICAN ☆

1

The Thunder on the Right

★★★★★

As the sun was going down upon the Eisenhower administration, something hit American politics broadside. Politicians were startled by the impact and the pundits are still busy explaining the force that caused the collision. Quite generally it is agreed that the force is a conservative upsurge, but such agreement is splintered by every effort neatly to define this conservatism and to describe its direction, duration and ultimate destination.

In a paraphrase of Thomas à Kempis, it is easier and perhaps better to feel this conservatism than attempt to define it. My own feeling about the phenomenon comes from close personal observations of its slow but steady development during the past twenty-five years. From its inception, the growing conservative movement has been a reaction that has not been permitted to react. It took form as a well-reasoned protest that has never had its day in the court of public opinion, precisely because its arguments have always been smothered at the crucial moments by an avalanche of circumstances contrived, timed and triggered by the ever resourceful defendants to this lawful popular complaint. From time to time, as it rolled down through the years, the conservative remonstrance has gained and lost an assortment of specific issues along with the influence of those who espoused them, but its main course has been firm and direct. The core of its complaint is as hard now as it was in the beginning and its adherents have finally snowballed into a majority of the American people.

Basically, the call of this persisting petition is for the restoration of the national independence and constitutional government of the United States. The issues that make up the conservative platform are all related directly or indirectly to this fundamental demand. In the first place, conservatives recognize that our national independence and constitutional government are a single issue, constituting the basic postulate of the conservative cause. Conservatives believe that this basic conjunction of national independence and constitutional government is the foundational underpinning of our national life. They allege that this supporting foundation has been virtually ignored for a quarter of a century and that the consequential progressive erosion of this underpinning now threatens to topple the whole superstructure of American freedom. Conservative concern is climaxed now in the general realization that if American freedom falls, all of that which goes by the name of Christian civilization will be suffocated in the resulting ruins.

It is in this sense that the cause of the present collision in American politics may properly be called a conservative movement and, by the same token, the millions who now clamor for this cause may properly be called "Conservatives."

Comes now the intellectual battle of words.[1] The theoreti-

---

1 "There are many signs to show that the English language is today endangered and degenerating. One of the signs is this: Samuel Johnson's dictionary is no longer in print, and has not been in print for decades. . . .

"Johnson's dictionary is full of shocks and surprises, as it reminds you what words originally meant; or sometimes, what they *should* mean. Take, for instance, the word 'conservative.' This has not been a popular word in recent times. Even some conservatives do not like the word; they think it is too nega-

cians are excited about the possibility that this militantly marching movement may be traveling under an improperly assumed name. Is this a truly conservative column, or is it in fact the reincarnation of eighteenth century liberalism? Are these people the true intellectual descendants of John Locke with an outcrossing to Edmund Burke, or are they imposters who trace their political ancestry no further back than Jay Gould, Grover Cleveland or even Calvin Coolidge? [2]

This debate will continue in the forums of the academic community and it should continue there, but the debate will have no appreciable effect upon the marching column of conviction that is now known as the "conservative upsurge." What faces the wavering American politician now is not a nebulous theory but a concrete condition. The modern conservative column was not formed to split a few political hairs, but to break an assortment of political heads. Basically, this movement is logical but its momentum is psychological and

---

tive, not aimed at action but suggesting immobility. But Johnson knew that conserving is an active and energetic discipline. In a world where things decline and dissipate in a thousand directions, one must have a clear set of ideas, and vast resources of will to make a complex thing like the American Constitution endure.

"For this reason there is nothing negative about Johnson's definition of the conservative. He defines the verb *to conserve* as 'to preserve without loss or detriment.' It is the ability to keep things pure, unmixed, unadulterated by time and its various taints. The adjective 'conservative' is defined with a vigor that makes the mind react as to trumpets: 'Conservative: having the power of opposing diminution or injury.'

"This is no word to be ashamed of. Conservatism is a *power* put at the disposal of a good thing that the human race needs. And it is a power forever threatened, forever opposing the pressures that make for diminution. What is in a word? Man's heart and hopes are put in words, and 'conservative' is a worthy receptacle for these treasures."

(*Chicago Tribune,* December 6, 1961. Guest editorial borrowed from the *Richmond News Leader,* Richmond, Virginia.)

[2] William F. Buckley, Jr. and Richard Hamowy in *The New Individualist Review,* November, 1961. "Do-it-Yourself Conservatism," *National Review,* January 30, 1962.

its across-the-board push can be identified as unapologetic, old-fashioned American patriotism that is angered beyond mere words.

The common denominator of the big mobilization is the determination to protect the American republic from a variety of assaults now being made against it. The advancing column is thoroughly conservative in the definitive sense of that term because it is dedicated to the conservation of the American heritage and the marchers are convinced that unless they move fast now on a broad political front, the American heritage is going to be destroyed by the deeply rutted, suicidal policies of their own government.

In American politics words stand for things, but even at their very best they stand unsteadily. Since 1932 our federal government has been managed by self-proclaimed "liberals." The advancing conservative column aims to unseat this prevailing liberalism precisely because its works prove that this "liberalism" is nothing more nor less than simon-pure statism. In its etymological root-sense, the word "liberal" means a devotee of freedom, and consequently liberals should be dedicated to liberation. However, since 1933,[3] the only thing the prevailing liberals have managed to liberate is the irresponsible force of our federal government. *Ipso facto,* this liberation has lighted the fuse for the destruction of our constitutional system which has proved to be *the most effective protection for human liberty ever devised by the brain and purpose of man.*

At this point, therefore, reference to deeds rather than words offers the only answer to two moot questions, namely, "Who is truly 'liberal'?" and "Who is authentically 'conservative'?"

But what about the "conservationists?" Throughout this angry debate "conservation" has managed to maintain its

[3] The repeal of the Eighteenth (Prohibition) Amendment, December 5, 1933.

"A" rating as a "good word." During the very same period that conservatives have been berated as cranky holdovers from the remote past who were vainly trying to turn back all the clocks of history, the word "conservationist" has called up the image of one who thinks long, wide and conscientiously about the rightful expectations of future generations. Now, as always, the conservationist is the vigilant maintenance man for the great store of natural resources with which our country has been endowed by God and nature. Conservation clubs for the preservation of forests, topsoil, water power and wild life are the common meeting grounds for all types of political activists from the far left to the radical right. Thus, all of the marchers in the approaching column of conservatives are authentic and enthusiastic conservationists with but one difference, namely, that the conservative marchers carry an enlarged inventory of national resources that now need to be conserved. Of course, the upsurging conservatives want to preserve our forests, fisheries and the rest, but their concern goes on beyond these physical and material assets to include a program for the conservation of those great spiritual and legal resources found in our Declaration of Independence and established in our American constitutional system.

The up-and-coming conservatives realize that without the constant support of these spiritual and legal resources, our material and physical assets could never have been developed or made to proliferate as they have—for the unprecedented prosperity of Americans and for the inspiration and advancement of all people everywhere. Impressed as all must be by the importance of our physical and material assets, conservatives nevertheless realize that these same things are found in profusion in many other countries of the world. But they realize too what many Americans forget, namely, that this is the only place on earth where human liberty has been protected by a constitutional government built upon the spiritual principles set forth in the American Declaration of Independence. In spite of the great physical and material resources of Soviet Russia, human liberty is dead in that country precisely because the Russian people are now deprived of the big spiritual and legal resources which the upsurging American conservatives are resolved to protect, restore and revitalize in the United States.

The modern conservative complaint against prevailing modern liberalism is thus a basic general allegation supported by an extended bill of particulars. Like their Founding Fathers before them, the current conservatives can and do cite "a long train of abuses and usurpations" which "evince a design to reduce them under absolute despotism." [4] Our generation too, has been made subject to a jurisdiction "foreign to our constitution and unacknowledged by our laws." [5]

The specifications in the conservative complaint are many and varied. There is acknowledged priority of urgency in many of these items and human differences of opinion among conservatives themselves about the pertinency of others. Nevertheless, conservatives have a firmly formed position on certain existing and/or threatened abuses and usurpations of power that seriously impinge upon our national independence and violate the limitations placed upon the federal government in the Constitution of the United States. There is conservative unity too on the positive side of the conservative case.

In spite of what you may have heard to the contrary, modern conservatives are militantly constructive and their construction will have the advantage of solid foundations, an advantage which the architects of modern liberalism have overlooked.

[4] The Declaration of Independence of the United States, 1776.
[5] *Ibid.*

There is room in this book for a limited discussion of a limited number of proposals that modern conservatives regard as vital to the cause of our national independence and constitutional government. But modern conservatism was not born yesterday. It has had a long past and its present program is the evolution of bitter experience. Conservatism is driven now by the expansive power of hot and heavy emotions that have been repressed, held down and blocked off for many years. To measure the present momentum of the movement, we must know where it started and how far and how fast it has moved to date. In short, before we can predict where current conservatism is going, we must know where it has been. For better or worse, the future of the movement will be the product of its past, for neither modern conservatism nor anything else can escape the exactions of its own history. The same can and must now be said of modern liberalism.

2

The Development of
Modern Liberalism

☆☆☆☆☆

The political progenitor of modern liberalism was Franklin D. Roosevelt. But the child was a bastard, for when F.D.R.
in person accepted the Democratic nomination at the 1932
Convention, he embraced "one hundred per cent" the thoroughly conservative platform that had just been adopted by
the party delegates. Throughout the campaign that followed
the Convention, Candidate Roosevelt supported that platform vigorously and effectively. One of the first recommendations that he sent to Congress as President was the Democratic promise to reduce federal expenditures by twenty-five
per cent.[1]

---

[1] The 1932 Democratic platform provided, in part:

"We believe that a party platform is a covenant with the people to be
faithfully kept by the party when entrusted with power, and that the people
are entitled to know in plain words the terms of the contract to which they
are asked to subscribe. We hereby declare this to be the platform of the
Democratic party:

"The Democratic party solemnly promises by appropriate action to put into
effect the principles, policies and reforms herein advocated, and to eradicate
the policies, methods and practices herein condemned. We advocate an immediate and drastic reduction of govermental expenditures by abolishing useless commissions and offices, consolidating departments and bureaus, and elim-
inating extravagances to accomplish a savings of not less than 25 per cent in
the cost of the federal government. And we call upon the Democratic party
in the states to make a zealous effort to achieve a proportionate result.

Congress responded promptly, and such a measure became law on March 20, 1933.[2] At this point, President Roosevelt broke off his attachment to the officially established principles and promises of his party and moved in with a coterie of ideological charlatans who had no obvious political background and who, for the most part, had not been publicly identified in his election campaign. It was from this miscellaneous association that modern liberalism was born.[3]

"We favor maintenance of the national credit by a federal budget annually balanced on the basis of accurate executive estimates within revenues, raised by a system of taxation levied on the principle of ability to pay.

"We advocate a sound currency to be preserved at all hazards and an international monetary conference called on the invitation of our government to consider the rehabilitation of silver and related questions.

"We advocate a competitive tariff for revenue with a fact-finding tariff commission free from executive interference, reciprocal tariff agreements with other nations, and an international economic conference designed to restore international trade and facilitate exchange.

"We advocate the extension of federal credit to the states to provide unemployment relief wherever the diminishing resources of the states makes it impossible for them to provide for the needy. . . .

"We advocate unemployment and old age insurance under state laws. . . . The removal of government from all fields of private enterprise except where necessary to develop public works and natural resources in the common interest."

[2] The so-called "Economy Act of 1933," Title 5 U.S.C. 26 et seq; Title 8 U.S.C. 117 et seq; Title 10 U.S.C 321 et seq. The salaries of all federal employees were cut by 15% and certain veterans' benefits were also cut. In 1934, these laws were repealed by the enactment of other laws restoring the cuts and raising both salaries and veterans' benefits in most cases.

[3] "Two camps grew up around Roosevelt with the politicians in one and the professors in the other. Relations between them were outwardly amicable, but the first group looked with considerable distaste and apprehension at the influx of professors. By and large the politicians assuaged their uneasiness by deciding that, after all, these 'theoreticians' like Tugwell and Berle could not count in the long run and had no relevance except in the innocuous field of speech-making. Later, when Roosevelt took them to Washington and tried to turn them into administrators, resentment grew. Louis Howe, in particular, held the Brain Trusters in something close to contempt, and one of Moley's jobs was to appease him and keep smooth relations between the rival camps.

For the sudden cancellation of his pledged plan of action, the President had the excuse of the deep economic depression, but he could not show any popular mandate for what he then proceeded to do, namely, to make the federal government a receiver in bankruptcy for the American economic system. The depression was full-blown during the campaign of 1932. President Hoover was the psychological victim of its impact and was foredoomed to defeat, regardless of what the Republican platform promised. Voters who believed that government intervention was the proper answer to the depression found no comfort in the Democratic platform[4] nor in the speeches of Democratic Candidate Roosevelt. But these people did have a very positive alternative.

In 1932, Mr. Norman Thomas was making his third successive race for President as the candidate of the Socialist party. At that time, when over ten million American workers were unemployed and all of our economic indices were on the down side, the Socialist platform presented such pledges as these to voters who believed that government intervention was the proper answer:

UNEMPLOYMENT

To relieve the tragic misery of millions of unemployed workers and their families we propose:

1. Immediate governmental relief of the unemployed by the extension of all public works and a program of long-range

---

The phrase, 'Brain Trust' came originally from Howe; he threw it off in irony as a term of ridicule. Then it was picked up by James Kieran of the *New York Times* and instantly caught on throughout the nation. FDR's own name for it—in the early days at least—was the 'Privy Council'."

Roosevelt in Retrospect, by John Gunther, (Harper and Brothers, New York, 1950,) p. 268.

4 See Chapter 2, Note, *supra.*

planning of public works following the present depression. All persons thus employed to be engaged at hours and wages fixed by bona fide labor unions.

2. Loans to states and municipalities without interest for the purpose of carrying on public works and the taking of such other measures as will lessen widespread misery.
3. A system of unemployment insurance.
4. The nation-wide extension of public employment agencies in cooperation with city federations of labor.

LABOR LEGISLATION

The lives and well-being of the producers and their families should be the first charge on society. We therefore urge:

1. A system of health and accident insurance and of old age pensions as well as unemployment insurance. As long as workers are dependent primarily upon their employers rather than on the community for protection against the exigencies of old age, sickness, accident and unemployment, employers hostile or indifferent to the labor movement will be able to use their private insurance schemes as powerful weapons against organized labor.
2. Shortening of the workday in keeping with the steadily increasing productivity of labor due to improvements in machinery and methods.
3. Securing to every worker a rest period of no less than two days in each week.
4. Enacting of an adequate federal anti-child-labor amendment.

TAXATION

For the proper support of government and as a step toward social justice we propose:

1. Increase of taxation on high income levels, of corporation taxes and inheritance taxes, the proceeds to be used for old-age pensions and other forms of social insurance. . . .

FARM RELIEF

The Socialist party believes that the farmer is entitled to special consideration because of the importance of agriculture, because of the farmers' present economic plight and because the farmer is unable to control the prices of what he buys and what he sells. Many of the party's demands, including public development of electrical energy, nationalization of coal and railroads, and reform of the credit system will be of distinct benefit to the farmer.

As a further means of agricultural relief, we propose:

1. Acquisition by bona fide cooperative societies and by federal, state and municipal governments of grain elevators, stockyards, storage warehouses, and other distributing agencies, and the conduct of these services on a non-profit basis.
2. Encouragement of farmers' cooperative purchasing and marketing societies and of credit agencies.
3. Social insurance against losses due to adverse weather conditions." [5]

In a hard-hitting, tireless campaign, Mr. Thomas made the most of these promises. He drew large and enthusiastic crowds wherever he appeared. Circumstances seemed to favor his cause. Much of the country was in an angry, rebellious mood. On the farms there were organized physical interferences with mortgage foreclosure proceedings and in the cities "unemployed councils" had set up headquarters which were rallying points for demonstrations, parades, and political

[5] *National Party Platforms, 1840-1960,* Univ. of Illinois Press, Urbana, Ill. 1961.

harangues. The Democratic high command became visibly worried about the possibility that Mr. Thomas would siphon off enough of the anti-Hoover votes from Roosevelt to permit President Hoover to end up with a majority in the electoral college. Official word came down to rank and file Democratic speakers to hammer Thomas' Socialist proposals as fantastic and Un-American. Distraught citizens were to be warned against wasting their votes by casting them for Thomas and Socialism.[6]

But when the popular votes were counted in November, 1932, Norman Thomas' total was 884,781, fewer than were cast for the Socialist candidate in 1912. Thus it was clearly demonstrated that in the deep trough of the great depression, when unemployment was at record heights and when our private enterprise system was in its deepest doldrums, the American voters nevertheless turned their backs squarely upon Socialism and government intervention. Instead they approved of a twenty-five per cent reduction in federal expenditures and voted their faith in Democrat Roosevelt's promise to reduce taxes.

Norman Thomas was disconsolate over his poor showing at what all regarded as such a propitious time for Socialism. He publicly declared:

"In such a revolutionary situation it was not merely or chiefly the Socialist vote which was smaller than one would expect. The Communist vote increased little over that of 1928. It will probably not exceed 75,000 for the whole country. . . . Yet the explanation must go deeper than this. There were all sorts of groups of American radicals and progressives who carefully eschewed the words 'Socialist' and 'Socialism.' They had programs or panaceas ranging all the way from the League for Independ-

[6] As an active member of the Speakers' Bureau of the Indiana State Democratic Committee in 1932, I personally received and disseminated this "official word."

ent Political Action's intellectualized version of a watered-down Socialism to 'Coin' Harvey's latest financial panacea. The times seemed ripe for them. . . .

"Yet not one of these groups made any impression on the electorate. . . . Did this collapse of minor parties mean that as in 1896 their ideas had captured one of the major parties? By no means. *Never in a time of depression did the principal candidate of the out's offer so little as Governor Roosevelt.* He won." [7] (Italics added.)

But Franklin D. Roosevelt came to have more faith in the future of American Socialism than Norman Thomas had. He promptly proceeded to scuttle the conservative Democratic platform, for which the American people had voted so overwhelmingly, and dedicated his administration to the enactment of socialist panaceas which those same voters had emphatically rejected. Whatever else may be said of this turnabout, it was, on its face, a flagrant repudiation of democracy.[8]

[7] Speech of Norman Thomas, *The Nation*, December 14, 1932, p. 584.

[8] On January 25, 1936, Alfred E. Smith, who was the Democratic party's candidate for President in 1928, made a speech in Washington. Among other things, he said:

"No administration in the history of the country came into power with a more simple, a more clear, or a more inescapable mandate than did the party that was inaugurated on the fourth of March, 1933. And no candidate in the history of the country ever pledged himself more unequivocally to his party platform than did the President who was inaugurated on that day. *Millions and millions of Democrats just like myself, all over the country, still believe in that platform.* What we want to know is why it wasn't carried out. . . .

"Study the record of the present administration up to date. Pick up the platform that more nearly squares with the record and you will put your hand on the Socialist platform. You don't dare touch the Democratic platform. . . . How do you suppose all this happened? Here is the way it happened. The young Brain Trusters caught the Socialists in swimming and they ran away with their clothes. It is all right with me if they want to disguise themselves as Norman Thomas, but what I won't stand for is to

The new Roosevelt moved fast, smashing precedent and promise with the same cavalier disdain. Each of his four immediate predecessors as President had refused to accord United States recognition to Soviet Russia. The reasons for this refusal had been well stated by Bainbridge Colby, Secretary of State in the administration of Woodrow Wilson, where Mr. Roosevelt had likewise served as Assistant Secretary of the Navy.

Here is what Mr. Colby said:

"It is not possible for the government of the United States to recognize the present rulers of Russia as a government with which the relation common to friendly governments can be maintained. This conviction has nothing to do with any particular political or official structure which the Russian people themselves may see fit to embrace. It rests upon a wholly different set of facts. These facts, which none disputes, have convinced the government of the United States, against its will, that the existing regime in Russia is based upon the negation of every principle of honor and good faith, and every usage and convention underlying the whole structure of international law; the negation, in short, of every principle upon which it is possible to base harmonious and trustful relations, whether of nations or of individuals. *The responsible leaders of the regime have freely and openly boasted that they are willing to sign agreements and undertakings with foreign powers while not having the slightest intention of observing such undertakings or carrying out such agreements.*

"This attitude of dishonoring obligations, voluntarily entered into, they base upon the theory that no compact or agreement made with a non-Bolshevist government can have any moral force for them. They have not only avowed this as a doctrine, but they have exemplified it in practice. Indeed, upon numerous occasions the responsible spokesman of this power, and its official agency,

---

let them march off under the banner of Jefferson, Jackson or Cleveland." (Italics added)

have declared that it is their understanding that the very existence of Bolshevism in Russia, the maintenance of their own rule, depends and must continue to depend, *upon the occurrence of revolutions in all other great civilized nations, including the United States, which will destroy and overthrow their governments and set up Bolshevist rule in their stead.*

"It is within the knowledge of this government of the United States that the Bolshevist government is itself subject to the control of a political faction with extensive international ramifications through the Third Internationale and that this body, which is heavily subsidized by the Bolshevist government from the public revenue of Russia, has for its openly avowed aim, the promotion of Bolshevist revolution throughout the world.

"The leaders of the Bolsheviki have boasted that their promise of non-intervention with other nations would in no wise bind the agents of this body. *There is no room for reasonable doubt that such agents would receive the support and protection of any diplomatic agency the Bolsheviki might have in other countries. Inevitably, therefore, the diplomatic service of the Bolshevist government would become a channel for intrigues and the propaganda of revolt against the institutions and laws of countries with whom it was at peace, which would be an abuse of friendship to which enlightened governments cannot subject themselves.*

"In the view of this government there cannot be any common ground upon which it can stand with a power whose conceptions of international relations are so entirely alien to its own, so utterly repugnant to its moral sense." [9] (Italics added.)

All of this was as true when Franklin D. Roosevelt became President as it is today. Nevertheless, on November 16, 1933, without so much as a "by your leave" to Congress or to the American people, the President, in the course of a midnight White House visit with Soviet emissary, Maxim Litvinov, casually signed a memorandum establishing diplomatic rela-

[9] Bainbridge Colby, Secretary of State, formal reply to an inquiry by the Italian ambassador as to recognition of Soviet Russia. Aug. 10, 1920.

tions with the Kremlin. At that moment, the Soviet slave system was in serious financial and political trouble.[10] At home and abroad it desperately needed the invigorating prestige that American recognition provided. For the conservatism to which Mr. Roosevelt was pledged "one hundred per cent" in 1932, this official legitimation of Soviet Communism proved to be the deepest and unkindest cut of all the wounds he inflicted upon it during the succeeding years of his life. Without this timely American recognition, Soviet Communism would have collapsed in ruins and its present challenge to the peace and freedom of the world would never have materialized.

But in 1933 President Roosevelt was completely insensitive to the dangers of both Socialism and Communism. His administration was being dominated by the one and deeply infiltrated by the other.[11] At the President's request, Congress quickly "rubber stamped" measure after measure which gave the Federal executive sweeping control over banking, agriculture and industry. In the short space of a few months, Presi-

---

[10] *A History of Russia*, by Jesse D. Clarkson (Random House Inc., New York, 1961.) pp. 582 et seq.

[11] "It is certain that, between the years 1930 and 1948, a group of almost unknown men and women, Communists or close fellow travelers, or their dupes, working in the United States government or in some singular unofficial relation to it, or working in the press, affected the future of every American now alive, and indirectly the fate of every man now going into uniform. Their names, with a half-dozen exceptions, still mean little or nothing to the majority of Americans; but their activities, if only in promoting the triumph of Communist China, have decisively changed the history of Asia, of the United States, and therefore of the world. If mankind is about to suffer one of its decisive transformations, if it is about to close its 2,000-year-old experience of Christian civilization, and enter upon another, wholly new and diametrically different, then that group may claim a part in history such as it is seldom given any man to play, particularly so few and such obscure men. One of them is Alger Hiss. . . ."

Witness, by Whittaker Chambers, (Random House Inc., New York, 1952,) p. 331.

dential authority over the lives, liberty and property of the American people was practically complete.[12]

Among other things, the unrestricted power of labor unions to organize freely without interference by employers or anti-trust laws had been made into a federal civil right. For this the union bosses would be duly and generously grateful at campaign time.[13] As a result of this consolidation of power, F.D.R. was political master of all that he surveyed. The Republicans were cowed and demoralized by the President's stinging invective in which he characterized all of his critics as "economic royalists."

The only effective opposition to the Roosevelt revolution was coming from the Supreme Court's interpretations of the United States Constitution.[14] The high-riding Chief Executive made no secret of his contempt for the "horse-and-buggy" mentality of the "Nine Old Men" who composed the Court at that time. His energetic White House "Brain Trust" made plans to remove this judicial obstruction in due course, but they were careful not to unfold these plans until all of the 1936 election returns were in.

Mr. Roosevelt won the 1936 election in a landside, and immediately unveiled his design to "pack the court" by in-

---

12 *The Roosevelt Revolution,* by Marie Einaudi, (Harcourt, Brace and Co., New York, 1959).

13 "The Roosevelt administration wanted to see organized labor grow. This attitude was based on a political estimate of union votes and the enormous increase in the power of union treasuries. On one occasion President Roosevelt telephoned John L. Lewis personally to ask for a large financial contribution to Senator Alben Barkley's campaign for re-election. At another time, he specifically named the sum to be contributed directly to his own campaign—$500,000. According to Lewis, he was given forty-eight hours to get the money."

Check-off by Jameson G. Campaigne, (Regnery & Co., Chicago, 1961) p. 7.

14 *Schechter Poultry Corp. v. U.S.* 295 U.S. 495, 1935. *U.S. v. Butler,* 297 U.S. 1, 1936.

creasing the number of Supreme Court judges, thus creating vacancies which he could fill with pliant "New Dealers."

For the first time since he took office, formidable opposition to the President developed in Congress, and after prolonged and heated controversy, the "packing plan" was killed.[15]

But the Supreme Court had had a close call. The hot breath of the violent debate fell upon the venerable body with a blighting power. The President had made his political point and the judges promptly acknowledged it. After the packing threat, the Court proceeded at once to give the green light to unlimited federal taxing, spending and regulating, its immediately preceding decisions to the contrary notwithstanding.[16]

---

[15] "At the time of the second inauguration, after Roosevelt had been given the oath of office by Chief Justice Hughes, the President was quoted as saying that he promised to support the Constitution; 'Yes, but it's the Constitution as I understand it, flexible enough to meet any new problem of democracy—not the kind of Constitution your Court has raised up as a barrier to progress and democracy.'

"On May 18, a few minutes after the President had received the letter of retirement of Justice Van Devanter, the Senate Judiciary Committee voted 10-8 that the court-packing bill should not pass.

"All in all, the court fight was a stunning defeat for the President. Whether or not it was a fatal or irretrievable one, however, depended on the events to follow. Two years later, with his eye on a string of pro-New-Deal court decisions, the President exulted that he had lost the battle but won the war." *Roosevelt, the Lion and the Fox,* by James McGregor Burns, (Harcourt, Brace and Co., New York, 1956) pp. 291 et seq.

[16] Throughout its history, up to the end of 1936, the Supreme Court had consistently barred federal legislation in economic matters as beyond the Court's jurisdiction. These decisions included *United Mine Workers v. Coronado Coal Co.* 259 U.S. 344 (1922); *Schechter Poultry Co. v. U.S.* 298 U.S. 495 (1935); *U.S. v. Butler,* 297 U.S. 1 (1936); *Carter v. Carter Coal Co.* 298 U.S. 238 (1936.)

The Due Process Clause had been used many times to upset federal attempts to regulate industries which were not affected with a public interest. *Lochner v. New York,* 198 U.S. 45 (1905); *Adkins v. Childrens Hospital,* 261 U.S. 525 (1923), and others.

After the 1936 election, it began to be obvious that federal intervention was not curing the economic depression. Elsewhere in the world, business was bounding back to normal, but in the United States in 1938, after a plethora of federal spending, lending, subsidizing and "pump-priming," more

---

The prevailing view of the Court up to 1936-1937 was that "its delicate and difficult office is to ascertain and declare whether the legislation is in accordance with or in contravention of, the provisions of the Constitution; and having done that, its duty ends." (*U.S. v. Butler,* supra.)

Beginning in the early part of 1937, the Court began to read fresh powers into the Constitution, and the experimental approach which had been characteristic of the federal government during the preceding four years suddenly found itself welcomed on the bench of the Supreme Court.

Among the first of these "New Deal" opinions was *NLRB v. Jones and Laughlin Steel Corp.,* 301 U.S. 1 (1937). The earlier and narrower interpretation of interstate commerce was abandoned and the Court said:

"We have often said that interstate commerce itself is a practical conception. It is equally true that interference with that commerce must be appraised by a judgment that does not ignore actual experience. . . . The fact that there appears to have been no major disturbances in that industry in the more recent period did not dispose of the possibilities of future and like dangers to interstate commerce which Congress was entitled to foresee and to exercise its protective power to forestall. . . ."

Soon after that, three Social Security cases settled the controversies over the federal power to tax and spend for the general welfare. Justice Cardoza explained the view of the Court in these words:

"Of the many available figures a few only will be mentioned. During the years 1929 to 1936, when the country was passing through a cyclical depression, the number of the unemployed mounted to unprecedented heights. . . . The fact developed quickly that the states were unable to give the requisite relief. The problem had become national in area and dimensions. There was need of help from the nation if the people were not to starve. It is too late today for the argument to be heard with tolerance that in a crisis so extreme the use of the moneys of the nation to relieve the unemployed and their dependents is a use for any purpose narrower than the promotion of the general welfare." (*Steward Machine Co. v. Davis,* 301 U.S. 548, 1937.)

Later on, in a case involving the old-age benefit clause of the Social Security Act, Cardoza again felt called upon to explain the Court's change of position:

than nine million American workers were still unemployed. The New Deal was splitting at the seams. In the face of obvious facts, the President's class-conscious ridicule of his opposition was losing its political pulling power. In 1938, the Republicans gained 81 seats in the House of Representatives, and this gave them a total of 170 in that body.

Under the ominous political circumstances, Mr. Roosevelt dropped the subject of his domestic reforms and turned to foreign affairs. He discovered the iniquities of Adolph Hitler and recalled our ambassador to Germany, William E. Dodd, on January 1, 1938. For good measure, he proposed an eco-

---

"Congress did not improvise a judgment when it found that the award of old-age benefits would be conducive to the general welfare. . . . A great mass of evidence was brought together supporting the policy which finds expression in the act. . . . The problem is plainly national in area and dimensions." (*Helvering v. Gerhardt*, 304 U.S. 405, 1938.)

In 1941, the Fair Labor Standards Act (Wage and Hour Law) was under fire, and in finding the Act valid, the Court, by that time unanimous, held that the powers delegated to the federal government cannot be limited in their exercise by the powers that the Constitution reserves to the states. Justice Stone spoke for the Court, in overruling *Hammer v. Dagenhart*, 247 U.S. 251, which had been the law since 1918:

"Congress, following its own conception of public policy concerning the restrictions which may appropriately be imposed on interstate commerce, is free to exclude from the commerce articles whose use in the states for which they are destined it may conceive to be injurious to the public health, morals or welfare, even though the state has not sought to regulate their use." (*U.S. v. Darby*, 312 U.S. 100, 1941.)

This change of position on the part of the Supreme Court is explained in *The Roosevelt Revolution*, supra, as follows:

"President Roosevelt was never in doubt for an answer. The change had been due to political pressure exercised on the Supreme Court, culminating with his plan for judicial reform. There is a great deal of validity in this answer." (ibid, page 219.)

The membership of the Court had not changed from 1932 to 1937. The last change had been in 1932 when Cardoza succeeded Holmes. Black was appointed to the Supreme Court in August, 1937.

nomic quarantine against Japan.[17] It soon became apparent that the President was prepared to win with war what he obviously was losing with peace, namely, the upcoming 1940 Presidential election.

In the first years of his administration, internationalists had criticized President Roosevelt for isolationism,[18] but they hailed his conversion now and moved in fast to help him fend off the impending showdown on the issue of domestic Socialism. Conservatives who had hoped to run the Constitution against the New Deal in 1940 were thus forced to fight the President on the field of his new-found foreign policy. When Hitler marched into Poland in September, 1939, the new issue was joined.

[17] Speech made by President Roosevelt in Chicago, October 5, 1938.
[18] *Roosevelt, The Lion and the Fox* by James MacGregor Burns, supra pp. 178 et seq.

3

Wars We Did Not Want

☆☆☆☆☆

The United States was dragged into both World Wars over a mountain of popular opposition. "He kept us out of war" was the rallying cry of Woodrow Wilson's re-election campaign in 1916.[1] Without the influence of this popular bromide, Wilson would certainly have been defeated. As it was, a political upset in California was all that saved the day for the Democrats in one of the closest Presidential contests in history.[2]

With election day only five months behind him, President

---

[1] On the night before the 1916 November election, Wilson partisans in front of Democratic Headquarters in Washington, D. C. were following a volunteer college cheer leader in the chant:

> "We want peace, we don't want war,
> We want Wilson four years more."

I was the cheer leader.

[2] The electoral vote was Wilson 277; Hughes, 254. Popular vote returns up to midnight of election day, November 7, 1916, indicated a Republican victory. Even the Democratic papers in the East conceded defeat. As the returns from the Midwest came in showing only Ohio for Wilson, the President privately admitted to a feeling of relief that the great burden of office had been lifted from him. Rejoicing Republicans serenaded Hughes at the Astor with two bands. Toward morning, however, when returns came in from the West, doubt as to the outcome succeeded the certainty of the night before. It was noon Thursday before the California returns confirmed the Wilson victory.

Wilson appeared before Congress on April 2, 1917, asking for a formalized declaration of what he called the war by Germany against the government and people of the United States. "The world must be made safe for democracy," said the President. Incidentally, this was the beginning of the use of "democracy" as a generic term in American polemics. Prior to Wilson's dramatic speech, "democracy" had been used here only in connection with the Democratic party. After World War I, the emergence of the new "democracies" in Europe gave a new twist to the American political vocabulary.[3]

[3] "Once upon a time the word 'democracy' may have meant the same thing to all who spoke and heard it. Today, however, it is such a limp and vapid expression that the Russian Foreign Minister and the chairman of the Republican National Committee can both praise it highly on the self-same afternoon.

"Any word that can be used at one and the same time to suggest the despotic political ideals of Soviet Russia and the treasured principles of Americanism has certainly lost every vestige of usefulness.

"The word 'democracy' has now become very much like the key to a highly exclusive private club which some waggish member caused to be secretly duplicated and widely distributed. Before the bona fide 'brothers' knew what was up, the plush and cosy clubhouse was swarming with all the questionable characters in the neighborhood. A disillusioned board of managers was finally forced to change the lock.

"Whatever significance may have been attached to it in the ancient past, the term 'democracy' is not now a dependable key to the secret of a free society. Its continued use simply serves to make existing 'confusion worse compounded,' by giving notoriously tyrannical despotism a distorted false face which seems to resemble American freedom. The friends and agents of these undeserving pretenders have given every encouragement to the currency of this word which dilutes the priceless and unique quality of Americanism by mixing and confusing it with the crude and forceful 'leveling' devices of European politics.

"The honest and serious students of American history will recall that our Founding Fathers managed to write both the Declaration of Independence and the Constitution of the United States without using the term 'democracy' even once. No part of any one of the existing state Constitutions contains any reference to the word. Such men as John Adams, Madison, Hamilton, Jefferson and others who were most influential in the institution and formation

Our entry into the European conflict was the event for which our "British" ambassador at the Court of St. James, Mr. Walter Hines Page, had been working notoriously for months.[4] Subsequent events proved that the American people were right and that President Wilson was wrong about the issues at stake in the war. Our involvement worked a tragic turn in our national history and it likewise marked an unfortunate day in the history of the whole world. We know now that in the absence of our participation, England would have compromised her differences with Germany and a resulting balance of European power might have preserved the peace of the world for a hundred years.[5]

Once the die was cast, President Wilson was determined to preserve future peace with a World Parliament. Having broken the ice of American isolation, he felt sure that the American people were ready to go the full distance into a League of Nations. Rebuffed in the United States Senate, he forced the issue into the 1920 elections which he said should be a "great and solemn referendum" on the League issue.[6]

In the Presidential election of 1920, the American people

---

of our government refer to 'democracy' only to distinguish it sharply from the republican form of our American Constitutional System."

The Key to Peace, by Clarence Manion, (Heritage Foundation, Chicago, 1950) pp. 48 et seq.

[4] *American Neutrality: 1914-1917,* by Charles Seymour, (Yale University Press, New Haven, Conn. 1935.)

Road to War: 1914-1917, by Walter Millis, (Houghton, Mifflin & Co. Boston, Mass.)

[5] *Propaganda for War* by H. C. Patterson (Univ. of Oklahoma Press, Norman, 1939.)

[6] President Wilson sent a letter to be read at the Jackson Day banquet at Washington, January 8, 1920, in which he said: "If there is any doubt as to what the people of the country think on this vital matter, the clear and only way out is to submit it at the next election to the voters of the nation, to give the election the form of a great and solemn referendum as to the part the United States is to play in completing the settlement of the war."

had their last chance to speak their mind directly on the question of our involvement in an internationalist organization. James M. Cox, the Democratic candidate, campaigned on a pro-League-of-Nations platform. Republican Warren G. Harding took the opposite side and promised a return to traditional standards of American "normalcy." [7] Harding won in a landslide and the internationalists learned a bitter but valuable lesson.[8] Never again did they make the mistake of permitting internationalist schemes to become the issue in a popular election. Henceforth, in order to "make the world safe for democracy" with American intervention, undemocratic devices and stratagems had to be invented. Conveniently for this purpose, the Supreme Court in 1920 came through with a decision that gave the internationalists what they were looking for, namely, a legal basis for making the provisions of international treaties and executive agreements immune from the strict limitations of traditional American Constitutional Law.[9]

In 1913 Congress had passed a law regulating the hunting of migratory birds. The Act purported to be an exercise of the constitutional power of Congress to regulate interstate and foreign commerce. The validity of the statute was challenged when a citizen of Kansas was arrested for violating the game laws by shooting from a motor boat. The defense was based on the provisions of the federal statute which provided a different date for the open season on wild ducks from

[7] Just before his nomination, Harding had stated his political creed in a speech before the Ohio Society of New York. "Stabilize America first, prosper America first, exalt America first."

[8] Harding carried every state of the North and West, all the border states except Kentucky and the southern State of Tennessee. "It was not a landslide", said President Wilson's secretary, Joseph Tumulty, "it was an earthquake."

[9] *Missouri v. Holland*, 252 U.S. 416, 1920.

the one specified in the state statute, and did not prohibit hunting from a motor boat. It was urged that the federal law superseded the conflicting state law.

The Supreme Court of Kansas decided that wild fowl were not an article of commerce within the meaning of the Constitution and that the congressional statute was therefore unconstitutional and void.[10] The decision was unpopular. Public sentiment favored adequate protection for migratory birds and this could not immediately be provided by a coordination of the game laws of the several states.

At this point a migratory bird treaty was concluded between the United States and Canada in which the two countries mutually pledged their sovereign efforts to protect the wild fowl that flew back and forth across their respective borders. When the treaty was concluded, Congress passed another statute with the expressed purpose of implementing and enforcing the Migratory Bird Treaty. The new law was in substantially the same terms employed by the previous statute that had been held unconstitutional in the McCullagh case (supra.)

A test case developed when the State of Missouri sued the United States game warden in the Federal Court to prevent the game warden from attempting to enforce the federal statute within the state. The suit was dismissed, and the judgment of dismissal was affirmed by the United States Supreme Court in 1920.[11]

Justice Holmes wrote the opinion in the landmark case and made a clear-cut distinction between the validity of a statute passed by Congress without the benefit of the treaty, and the one then before the court, *passed pursuant to the treaty provisions*. The opinion stated:

10 *State v. McCullagh et al,* 96 Kans. 786, 1915.
11 *Missouri v. Holland,* 252 U.S. 416, 1920.

"An earlier act of Congress that attempted, by itself and not in pursuance of a treaty, to regulate the killing of migratory birds within the states had been held bad in the district court. (*United States v. Shauver*, 214 Fed. 154; *United States v. McCullagh*, 221 Fed. 288.) Those decisions were supported by arguments that migratory birds were owned by the states in their sovereign capacity, for the benefit of their people, and that under cases like *Geer v. Connecticut*, 161 U.S. 519 . . . this control was one that Congress had no power to displace. The same argument is supposed to apply now with equal force.

"*Whether the two cases were decided rightly or not, they cannot be accepted as a test of the treaty power. Acts of Congress are the supreme law of the land only when made in pursuance of the Constitution, while treaties are declared to be so when made under the authority of the United States.* It is open to question whether the authority of the United States means more than the formal acts prescribed to make the convention. *We do not mean to imply that there are no qualifications to the treaty-making power, but they must be ascertained in a different way. It is obvious that there may be matters of the sharpest exigency for the national well-being that an act of Congress could not deal with, but that a treaty, followed by such an act could, and it is not lightly to be assumed that, in matters requiring national action 'a power which must belong to and somewhere reside in every civilized government,' is not to be found.*

". . . The treaty in question does not contravene any prohibitory words to be found in the Constitution. *The only question is whether it is forbidden by some invisible radiation from the general terms of the 10th Amendment. . . .*

". . . Valid treaties, of course, 'are as binding within the territorial limits of the states as they are effective throughout the domination of the United States. . . .' *No doubt the great body of private relations usually falls within the control of the state, but a treaty may override its power. . . .*" (Italics added.)

The Supreme Court affirmed the decision of the lower court in dismissing the action. What *Missouri v. Holland* affirmed in effect was the right of the President with the advice and consent of the Senate, to make an agreement with a foreign nation or group of nations that would effectively substitute the provisions of the treaty for the existing laws of the several states. Justice Holmes spoke of "invisible radiation from the general terms of the 10th (States' rights) Amendment." Nevertheless the radiations from his revolutionary decision were clearly visible to the internationalists. The *Missouri v. Holland* decision meant that all "States rights" could be sidetracked by international treaties, and, as it was later decided by the Supreme Court, by simple Executive Agreements between the President and the heads of foreign states.[12]

The Executive Agreement might be secret—"classified," so to speak—and so unannounced to the public or to Congress. Thus the unique federal feature of our American government which had made the states just as supreme in the

12 *U.S. v. Pink*, 315 U.S. 203, 1941.

That was an action brought by the United States to recover the assets of the New York branch of the First Russian Insurance Company which remained in the hands of the respondent after the payment of all domestic creditors. Discussing the similarity between an ordinary treaty and an Executive Agreement, which was involved in the case, the Court said:

"If the priority had been accorded American claims by treaty with Russia, there would be no doubt as to its validity. . . . The same result obtains here. The powers of the President in the conduct of foreign relations included the power, *without consent of the Senate,* to determine the public policy of the United States with respect to the Russian nationalization decrees. 'What government is to be regarded here as representative of a foreign sovereign state is a political rather than a judicial question. . . .' As we have noted, this Court in the Belmont case recognized that the Litvinov Assignment was an international compact which did not require the participation of the Senate. . . . (Quoting from the Belmont case, 301 U.S. 331) *'In respect of all international negotiations and compacts, and in respect of our foreign relations generally, state lines disappear. As to such purposes the State of New York does not exist.'* " (Italics added.)

area of their reserved powers as the federal government was in the domain delegated to it in the Constitution, could now be disregarded at the pleasure of the President by an agreement with a foreign power.

To be valid and binding, the laws of Congress must be passed "in pursuance of" the Constitution, that is to say, the law must be respectful of the division of powers between the state and the federal governments and be otherwise consistent with all stipulations and requirements of the "Supreme Law of the Land." But a treaty, and now an Executive Agreement, need only to be made "under the authority of the United States." [13] That being done, the provisions of the treaty or Executive Agreement supersede all existing laws, state or federal.[14]

The revolutionary implications of these new "radiations" from *Missouri v. Holland* were not immediately impressed upon the people of the United States. A popular reaction into isolationism had followed the end of World War I, and internationalism went into a temporary eclipse.

When Franklin D. Roosevelt assumed the Presidency in 1933, he was engrossed in domestic affairs.[15] It was 1938 when he first served the American people with notice that once more we were about to become involved with the wars of Europe and Asia. At that time, Stalin had moved his Soviet communist commissars into direct control of the Loyalist side in the bloody Spanish Civil War. Hitler and Mussolini were siding with the anti-Communist forces of General Franco.

[13] Article VI, section 2, United States Constitution.

[14] Congress may pass a statute *subsequent* to the treaty, overruling the treaty provisions. Whichever is last in point of time, the treaty or the Congressional law, is supreme. (*Ribas v. U.S.* 194 U.S. 315) This rule does not apply, of course, to treaties that are not self-executing, but which require a subsequent act of Congress to give the treaty effect.

[15] London Economic Conference proceedings, 1933.

France and England were maintaining a nervous neutrality. For years both countries were in a quandary as to what they should do about Adolf Hitler. Although both France and England had made formal gestures of friendship in the direction of the Soviet Union, "great financial and commercial interests of the western Democracies, including many in the United States, were firm in the belief that war between the Soviet Union and Hitlerite Germany could only be favorable to their own interests. They maintained that Russia would necessarily be defeated and with this defeat Communism would be destroyed; also that Germany would be so weakened as a result of the conflict that for many years thereafter she would be incapable of any real threat to the rest of the world." [16]

Burnett Bolloten, United Press correspondent in Spain during the Civil War, has documented this fateful debate about Hitler in his important book, *The Grand Camouflage —The Communist Conspiracy in the Spanish Civil War.*[17] Bolloten concludes:

"That the rulers of Western Europe were confronted with a fateful choice is indubitable: On the one hand, they could oppose and destroy the Nazi regime while it was still weak, leaving the Soviet Union free to develop its resources and become in time, with allied Communist parties, the greatest menace in the world; on the other hand, they could, though not without opprobrium and extreme peril to themselves, allow the Nazi regime to overrun the non-totalitarian states in Central and Southeastern Europe lying west of Russia's border in the hope that it would in time come into collision with the rising power of the Soviet Union . . .[18]

[16] *The Time for Decision* by Sumner Welles, (Harper and Brothers, New York, 1944).
[17] *The Grand Camouflage* by Burnett Bolloten, (Frederick A. Praeger, New York, 1961).
[18] *Ibid* p. 92

"What Moscow wants, ran an article, September 24, 1936, that was typical of an appreciable segment of French opinion, 'is a war between French and German soldiers. At some time or another, on some pretext or another, Russia hopes that she will be able to force us (France) to throw our troops against the German frontier and deal a double blow by weakening the dreaded German power and by delivering our country up to a foreign war, which would ring in the hour of the Bolshevik Revolution.' " [19]

This prolonged and fateful debate which took place in Europe between 1936 and 1939 was plainly audible in Washington. In those days there was no direct and private wire connecting the White House with No. 10 Downing Street as there is now. Nevertheless, Winston Churchill even before he got there never let Franklin D. Roosevelt forget that for better or worse, come what might, Britain and the United States were in the debate together and on the same side. [20]

But as in 1915, 1916 and 1917, the big stumbling-block in the way of complete British-United States co-operation was the great majority will of the American people to remain aloof from the war in Europe. A reporter for the American Academy of Political and Social Science wrote in 1937:

[19] *Ibid,* p. 96. It will be remembered that Molotov for Stalin and Von Ribbentrop for Hitler, signed a pact of friendship between Nazi Germany and Soviet Russia on August 29, 1939 which divided Poland between them and thus forced France to throw her troops against the German frontier on September 3.

[20] The fact that President Roosevelt and Winston Churchill secretly exchanged "a stream of information" beginning in September, 1939, and continuing until the United States entered the war was admitted by Mr. Churchill himself in a public speech reported in the *London Times,* April 18, 1945 The question of this secret correspondence (1939-1941) was raised in the United States Senate on June 19, 1944, with the inference that in this correspondence President Roosevelt had promised that the United States would come to the aid of Great Britain in its war with Germany.

President Roosevelt and the Coming of the War, by Charles A. Beard, (Yale University Press, New Haven), pp. 265, 295.

"There is one point upon which an overwhelming majority of Americans are agreed today. That is that if war comes to Europe and/or Asia, this country should keep out of it. . . . Considerable acquaintance with popular opinion in many parts of the nation convinces me that anti-war sentiment is overwhelmingly in the majority. *The man in the street is convinced that our intervention in the last war was a ghastly error; that the ideals for which we fought were betrayed by our cynical allies; that those allies defrauded us out of money loaned them in their hour of need and that no good would come out of our participation in a suicidal struggle in which we have no personal interest.*" [21]

The "man in the street" was not interested in foreign wars but his increasing interest in the failure of the New Deal to cure unemployment and promote prosperity encouraged the impatient conservatives as much as it alarmed and irritated President Roosevelt. The Democratic Party was no longer responding to New Deal discipline. Publisher William Allen White wrote to National Chairman Farley:

"If our beloved leader cannot find the least common multiple between John L. Lewis and Carter Glass [United States Senator from Virginia], he will have to take a maul and crack the monolith, forget that he had a party and build his policy with the pieces which fall under his hammer." [22]

White's letter called for a Presidential invitation to a new Liberal-New Deal party from which the Carter Glasses would be rigidly excluded. The fact that it was addressed to adamantean Democrat Farley was ironical. F.D.R. was not ready to follow the example of his distinguished cousin Theodore. He was confident that he could find a suitable common de-

[21] *Annals of the American Academy of Political and Social Science,* July, 1937, Vol. 192, p. 42. (*Italics added.*)
[22] Quoted in *The Lion and the Fox,* by James McGregor Burns, (Harcourt Brace & Co., New York), p. 378.

nominator for his diversified supporters but he was determined not to make it large enough to accommodate the likes of Carter Glass. To begin with, he would simply get rid of the recalcitrants. And so in the primary elections of 1938 the President merely waved the big maul while he launched his famous purge of unfaithful Democrats.

Publicly, officially, and ruthlessly, the full weight of the National Administration's wide and comprehensive influence was thrown into an all-out effort to defeat its foes and elect the pliant friends of the New Deal. The noisy effort failed miserably. Big labor organizations stayed with the President, but that was not enough. Most of Mr. Roosevelt's friends were defeated for re-nomination or re-election while all of his foes, with the sole exception of Representative John O'Connor of New York, returned to Washington in triumph. Conservatives rejoiced and looked toward 1940 with the confident expectation of burying the New Deal, lock, stock and barrel.

But the 1938 "trial run" convinced the wily politician in the White House that he must shift his stance if he was to hold his lease. The converging crises in world affairs gave the President the opening he needed for an expedient maneuver. A Rome-Berlin-Tokyo Axis had been formally established in 1937. British Prime Minister Chamberlain was gambling on the hope that Hitler would leave the West in peace while he took off after Stalin. When the Germans annexed Czechoslovakia in March, 1939, Mr. Chamberlain's hope became very pale. Roosevelt responded by having Sumner Welles proclaim for our State Department against "acts of lawlessness." In April the President himself appealed to Hitler and Mussolini to cease, desist and confer but at the same time he re-asserted our determination to enter no entanglements and make no foreign commitments. Hitler rebutted by telling Mr. Roosevelt to quit worrying about the whole world.

The President was outpointed in that interchange, but only momentarily, for with June came the British King and Queen for a spectacular "visit of friendship" to the United States. Every moment of this extravaganza was arranged, stage-managed and glamorized under the personal direction of President Roosevelt himself.

The final "Auld Lang Syne" sung by the waving crowd of well-wishers as the royal couple rode out of Hyde Park had an ominous ring. Shadows cast by coming events were then discernible to all who cared to look. To the people with memories that ran back as far as Sarajevo in 1914, the picture looked like the place where they came in.

It did indeed, for in August, 1939, the U.S.S.R. and Germany signed their "non-aggression pact" of friendship, thus killing the hopes of those who, like Neville Chamberlain and Ambassador Joseph P. Kennedy, had believed that Hitler and Stalin could be made to accommodate the West by killing each other off. The Hitler-Stalin accord cleared the road to war, and on September 1st, the Germans invaded Poland which both France and Britain had agreed to protect. Thus both of these countries were in the war from its outset. Molotov, the Soviet Foreign Minister, then made a speech in which he declared that Poland had ceased to exist, therefore all Polish-Russian treaties were dead. A million Soviet soldiers immediately moved into Poland from the East and met the Germans in the middle of that country which, then and there, the Nazis and Communists split up between them. For Hitler and Stalin the new World War was a joint venture for common conquest, and they promptly shared its first ill-gotten gains, namely, Poland.

From this time forward all of our domestic political issues

were heavily blanketed by the overriding question of war or peace for the United States.

In 1939, not even the most rabid anti-Hitler or pro-British agitator in this country was brash enough to advocate war against the dictators. On the contrary, all of the early "interventionist" committees that formed in the United States professed to be for "peace." One of these which appeared in 1939, led by Clark Eichelberger and others, called itself The Non-Partisan Committee for Peace by Revision of the Neutrality Act. Interventionist peace-preservers wanted to begin by repealing our official neutrality and thus enabling the United States to aid the allies (Britain and France) by methods "short of war."

After Hitler's invasion of Poland, President Roosevelt invoked a special session of Congress to repeal the legally established arms embargo and permit all kinds of goods to be sold to all belligerents as long as title was taken by them in the United States and transported abroad in foreign ships. This came to be known as the "cash-and-carry" plan. On its face, it was nondiscriminatory but in fact it aided those belligerent countries which had the ships, such as Britain and France, and hurt the one that did not, namely, Germany.

Soon came the Committee to Defend America by Aiding the Allies, with William Allen White as chairman, and Clark Eichelberger as executive director.

This committee quickly developed a semiofficial status as a public sounding board for President Roosevelt's foreign policies. In this role it enjoyed the full support of the State Department and other federal agencies which gave it a tremendous impact upon American public opinion.

When Hitler's forces swept through the European democracies in April, May and June, it became obvious that 1940 would not be the year of decision between the Roosevelt New Deal and a regenerated American conservatism. The country was now split down the middle on "How much Aid to the Allies?" and "What is 'Short of War'?" The Johnson Act barred loans to belligerents but it did not prevent President Roosevelt from "exchanging" fifty "overaged" American destroyers for the right of the United States to establish military bases on British possessions in the western hemisphere. At the same time, the America First Committee was formed *to defend America by keeping the United States out of the European war.* Thenceforth, American public opinion was polarized with the "interventionists" on one side, and "America Firsters" on the other. In general, the conservatives lined up against intervention, while the chronic internationalists and liberals like Eichelberger and William Allen White took the other side.

But there were many important exceptions to this general rule. For instance, hard knots of organization and articulation were tied together upon the basis of prejudice against one side of the war or the other, with little or no consideration for what was good for the United States.

Some professional anti-Semites wanted the anti-Semitic Hitler to win and this encouraged influential Jewish organizations to plump hard for his defeat. All the while that Hitler and Stalin were allies, American Communists took a strong stand against our intervention. Because of his obvious attempts to help the Allies in 1939 and 1940, the Communists called President Roosevelt an "imperialist war-monger" or worse.[23] But when Hitler invaded Russia (June 22, 1941) American Communists immediately switched to the interventionist side and thereafter worked energetically to bring this country into the war against Germany and Japan.

[23] In February, 1940, President Roosevelt had said: "The Soviet Union, as everybody who has the courage to face the fact knows, is run by a dictatorship as absolute as any other dictatorship in the world. It has allied itself with another dictatorship." *Public Papers,* 1940 Vol. p. 9.

As soon as Hitler's forces knifed into Russia, the German ambassador in Tokyo was instructed to bring pressure upon the Japanese government to declare war against the Soviet Union and follow up the declaration with an invasion of Siberia. Soviet officials were terrified at this prospect and their agents in Japan worked feverishly to persuade Japan to turn South instead of North.

When the Tokyo government decided to follow the Russian advice (July 2), Soviet spies flashed the word to the Kremlin and the Red Siberian forces were immediately transferred to the western front to help hold back the Hitler invasion. But the Soviets could never be insured of immunity from a "two front" (Japanese-German) attack as long as the United States and Japan were at peace. Nothing short of war between this country and Japan could draw the Japanese troops permanently away from the vulnerable Soviet Siberian frontier. By the same token, the Communists knew that the ultimate defeat of Japan and the destruction of its military power would open China and the continent of Asia for Communist conquest. It is not surprising, therefore, to find that the Soviet spy apparatus had a firm hand in events that led to the Japanese strike at Pearl Harbor on December 7, 1941.[24] We know now that this or some attack by Japan was confidently expected by the White House. Historical research during the past twenty years has distilled every element of "surprise" from the beginning of our war with Japan.[25]

[24] See *Communism at Pearl Harbor,* by Anthony Kubek, (University of Dallas, Teacher Publishing Company, Dallas, Texas, 1962).

[25] "Neither Roosevelt nor Hull believed that the Japanese would accept the terms embodied in the American note of November 26 (1941). Why then did they submit it? Could it be that they meant to provoke Japan to attack the United States so that the latter might get into war with Germany by the back door? This is the thesis followed by some of our best historians today." (Kubek, supra, p. 21)

In his diary for November 25, 1941, Secretary of War Stimson noted:

"At the White House meeting were Hull, Knox, Marshall, Stark and myself. The President brought up entirely the relations with the Japanese. He brought up the event that we were likely to be attacked, perhaps (as soon as) next Monday, for the Japanese are notorious for making an attack without warning and the question was what we should do. *The question was how we should maneuver them into the position of firing the first shot without allowing too much danger to ourselves.*" (Italics added) *Quoted by* Charles A. Beard in *President Roosevelt and the Coming of War,* (Yale Univ. Press, 1948), p. 517.

Later, General Wedemeyer was to add to this:

"President Roosevelt had maneuvered us into the war by his patently unneutral actions against Germany and the final ultimatum to Japan. . . . On December 4, 1941, we received definite information from two independent sources that Japan would attack the United States and Britain but would maintain peace with Russia. . . . On December 6, our intercepts told us that the Japanese were going to strike somewhere the very next day. President Roosevelt had ample time to broadcast a warning which might have caused the Japanese to call off their surprise attack. At any event, we would not have permitted 3500 Americans to die at Hawaii without an opportunity to fight back." [General Albert C.] *Wedemeyer Reports,* (Henry Holt and Company, New York, 1958, pp. 2-3, 429-430).

Husband E. Kimmel, United States Navy Rear Admiral, was Commander-in-Chief of the Pacific Fleet at Pearl Harbor at the time of the Japanese attack on December 7, 1941. On December 7, 1958, the author interviewed Admiral Kimmel, then retired, on the radio network of the Manion Forum. Among other things, Admiral Kimmel said:

"I believe those who had seen the intercepted and decoded Japanese messages including the fourteen-part message received on December 6, and December 7, 1941, knew war with Japan was inevitable and the almost certain objective of the Japanese attack would be the fleet at Pearl Harbor. Those, among others, who saw the intercepted Japanese messages as they were received included the President; the Secretary of State, Mr. Hull; the Secretary of War, Mr. Stimson; the Secretary of the Navy, Mr. Knox; the Chief of Staff of the Army, General Marshall. . . . When Mr. Roosevelt had read the thirteen parts about 9:00 P.M. on December 6, 1941, he remarked: 'This means war.' All the investigations of the disaster have failed to disclose where General Marshall spent the evening of December 6, 1941, or what he did. In 1957, I received information which I believe to be reliable that the British subject serving in the Chinese government as Commissioner of Education and Intelligence in China received on November 30, 1941, from his intelligence sources in Japan, information of the planned attack on Pearl Harbor to be launched on December 7; where the Japanese fleet would congregate to launch the planes; the hour the planes were to be launched; the berths of the United States fleet in Pearl Harbor, and which ships were to be bombed first. This information was sent to London in a coded message on Sunday, November 30, or Monday, December 1, 1941. Whether the Chinese Commissioner's intelligence was transmitted from London to Washington, I do not know, but it appears highly probable that it was made available to Mr. Roosevelt. If Mr. Roosevelt did in fact receive the Chinese Commissioner's intelligence it was merely a detailed confirmation of the inevitable conclusion to be reached from an evaluation of the intercepted Japanese messages already available to him. *My belief is that General Short and I were not given the information available in Washington and were not informed of the impending attack because it was feared that action in Hawaii might deter the Japanese from making the attack."* (Manion Forum Broadcast No. 219, December 7, 1958, Manion Forum, South Bend, Indiana.) [26]

A recent volume provides further enlightenment:

"On November 27, 1941, the President sent his son, James Roosevelt, to Stephenson (a secret British agent) with a special message, the purport of which was not as yet known either to the British Foreign Office or to the British Embassy in Washington. The same same day Stephenson telegraphed it to London. His telegram read: 'Japanese negotiations off. Services expect action within two weeks.'

"Another urgent cable was sent from London, this time to Stephenson informing him that the Prime Minister and the Cabinet would be most interested to know the source of his information. Stephenson answered briefly: 'The President of the United States.'" *Room 3603*, by H. Montgomery Hyde (Farrar, Straus and Co., New York, 1963, p. 213.)

[26] For a complete account of the Pearl Harbor intercepted messages and other circumstances immediately preceding the December 7, 1941, attack see *Back Door to War: The Roosevelt Foreign Policy: 1933-1941* by Charles C. Tansill (Regnery and Co., Chicago, 1952); *Pearl Harbor—The Story of the Secret War"* by George Edward Morgenstern, (The Devin-Adair Co., New York, 1947); *Admiral Kimmel's Story* by Husband E. Kimmel, (Regnery and Co., Chicago, 1955); *The Final Secret of Pearl Harbor* by Robert A. Theobald, (The Devin-Adair Co., New York, 1954).

In view of what had been transpiring since election day, 1940, the President's anxiety for an overt provocation from Japan is understandable. He had baited Hitler for an attack without success and his attempts to exploit German submarine encounters with our convoying destroyers in the Atlantic had left the country cold.[27] The President knew, and those around him knew, that by November, 1941, the non-interventionists had fought him to a standstill. This country did not want the war in which Mr. Roosevelt had determined to involve it. He was at his wits' end.[28]

If the Japanese had been deterred from making this December 7 attack as Admiral Kimmel states that they should have been, subsequent history could have taken off in a radically different direction. On November 1, 1941, the big and growing America First organization had held a national convention in Washington, D. C. The keynoter, former Governor Philip Lafollette of Wisconsin, pictured the impending Congressional elections as a clash between the "War Party" and the "American Party." "We leave this hall tonight," he said, "with our coats off and our sleeves rolled up. We are headed for the 1942 elections. We have only two planks in our platform: The Declaration of Independence and the Constitution of the United States." But, conveniently for the "Great White Father" of modern liberalism and more recently the standard bearer of the new internationalism, the "treacherous" Japanese intervened.

[27] *President Roosevelt and the Coming of the War,* Beard, (supra) Chapter V, p. 133 et seq.

[28] "The truth was that, as the world situation became more desperately critical, and as the limitless peril came closer and closer to the United States, isolationist sentiment became ever more strident in expression and aggressive in action and Roosevelt was relatively powerless to combat it. He had said everything 'short of war' that could be said. He had no more tricks left. The hat from which he had pulled so many rabbits was empty." *Roosevelt and Hopkins* by Robert Sherwood (Harper & Brothers, New York, 1948), pp. 382-383.

On December 11, 1941, the America First National Committee met in Chicago and dissolved the organization by formal resolution which read in part: "Our principles were right. Had they been followed war could have been avoided. No good purpose can now be served by considering what might have been had our objectives been attained. We are at war. Today, though there may be many important subsidiary considerations, the primary objective is victory." That being done, retired Army General Robert E. Wood, the National Chairman of America First, upon motion, gavelled the organization out of existence and left the meeting to rejoin the nation's armed forces. The United States had a war to win. Subsidiary considerations, such as the Declaration of Independence and the Constitution of the United States would have to wait.

4

An Election Without a Choice:
Roosevelt v. Willkie

☆☆☆☆☆

In the summer of 1939, "explosion after smoky explosion blew away Franklin D. Roosevelt's last vestige of control over both Houses of Congress." [1] A combination of Congressional conservatives, "Republicrats," so-called, were riding herd on the New Deal, and its resourceful leader in the White House appeared to be cornered at last. Anti-administration Democrats were relying upon the "no third term" tradition to get rid of FDR in their 1940 convention, and the conservative Republicans were increasingly confident of success in the 1940 elections, regardless of what happened in the Democratic contest for the Presidential nomination.

Publicly, the President went on record repeatedly with an expressed desire to lay down the burdens of his high office and retire to the tranquil shades of his beloved Hyde Park, but the political professionals never took these rhapsodic effusions any more seriously than Mr. Roosevelt himself did. In retrospect we are sure now that, long before 1939, the President had decided to run again in 1940 if his chances for re-election appeared at that time to be better than even. The stark possibility of defeat was galling to the President's vanity. This was the only effective deterrence to his interior

[1] *Time Magazine*, July 31, 1939, p. 8

resolution, and it haunted him up to the eleventh hour of election night.[2]

Roosevelt wanted to be drafted by the Party convention and then swept into office by a great popular majority. Thus, history would record that not even the great George Washington himself could have resisted such an appeal from the grateful hearts of his countrymen.

It did not work out exactly as FDR had wished, but the distinctions between fancy and fact made no appreciable difference, except to the evaluations of history. Roosevelt could dream, of course, but in essence he was the most practical of practical politicians. In the summer of 1939 he knew that, as of then, he was licked; if Adolph Hitler had managed to control his psychopathic urges for conquest, at least for the time being, Roosevelt would have retired gracefully in 1940 and willed his battered New Deal to the tender mercies of his Republican enemies. But the President was confident that Hitler would soon make war and, in so doing, make Roosevelt the indispensable man for the United States in 1940. The conservative coalition in Congress, the "Republicrats," were equally confident that there would be no war in Europe, but they hedged this conviction with frequent

[2] "The early returns were mixed. . . . Suddenly, Mike Reilly, the President's bodyguard, noticed that Roosevelt had broken into a heavy sweat. Something in the returns had upset him.

" 'Mike,' Roosevelt said suddenly, 'I don't want to see anybody in here.' 'Including your family, Mr. President?' 'I said *anybody*,' Roosevelt answered in a grim tone.

"Roosevelt sat before his charts. Was this the end of it all? Better by far not to have run for office again than to go down in defeat now—all his personal enemies gathered in one camp. . . . Would this strange coalition at last knock him down and write his epitaph in history as a power-grasping dictator rebuked by a free people?"

(*Roosevelt, the Lion and the Fox,* by James MacGregor Burns, (Harcourt, Brace, and Co., New York, 1956) p. 452.

statements that if such a war did come, we should remain aloof from it. These "isolationists" believed that the President was under the influence of a group of American Anglophiles who were flooding the country with interventionist propaganda.

Said Senator Robert A. Taft:

"No one has ever suggested before that a single nation should range over the world . . . protecting democracy. . . . Such a policy is not only vain but almost inevitably leads to war. Now it is suggested that the whole world is different. It is said that distances are so short we cannot possibly avoid being involved in a general war. I don't believe it. It seems essential that the President shall not have discretion to take sides in foreign wars or to impose sanctions against those nations which he might find to be aggressive nations. [Congress] should not permit the Executive to go too far towards war without consulting Congress." [3]

Senator Arthur Vandenberg, like Taft, a leading Republican Presidential "hopeful," was talking in the same vein. Said he:

"Protected by a great ocean on either side, the United States need fear no other nation if we mind our own business, concentrate our attention on domestic problems of our own and decline to surrender to the propaganda that we cannot escape participation in other peoples' wars. Our challenge is not abroad, it is at home." [4]

These and other declarations by ambitious conservative leaders reflected the general confidence that the New Deal could and would be vanquished in 1940 if the election was made to turn strictly upon the domestic record of the Roosevelt administration. The President's political enemies were

[3] *Vital Speeches,* February 1, 1939, p. 254.
[4] *New York Times,* June 6, 1939.

sure that he was well aware of this and would therefore "move heaven and earth" to turn the 1940 campaign into a debate on foreign policy. For practical reasons, therefore, all leading Republican conservatives were outspoken "isolationists" in 1939.

Thus it soon became obvious to interventionists that, in the normal course of events, the Republicans would nominate an isolationist for President in 1940 who would probably win the election the following November, unless in the meantime the European crisis exploded into a war which so seriously threatened American interests that domestic issues would be completely eclipsed.

Like President Roosevelt, interventionists were convinced that a European war was coming, but they could not predict when it would start or how long it would go on before the United States could become actively involved. With Roosevelt as President they were confident that our intervention would follow with all possible speed, but they realized too that if Roosevelt should be defeated in 1940 by a determined isolationist, the United States might never be pulled into the European conflict. Against this frightful possibility, the interventionists needed insurance. They could obtain it only by bringing about the nomination of an interventionist in the 1940 Republican convention. In 1939, the chances for such an achievement were bleak, to say the least. Every man then being seriously mentioned as a possible Republican nominee was an isolationist with his noninterventionist views as deeply dyed as those of Taft and Vandenberg. But the stakes were high and the internationalists were undaunted by the big odds against them.

In the years since 1939, conservative Americans have learned that they must never underestimate the power of the internationalists to manipulate Presidential nominations.

This education was begun in the early dawn of 1940. During 1939, a few "timid feelers" had been circulated concerning a man named Wendell Willkie who, in 1936, had served with James A. Farley as a member of the Tammany County Democratic Committee in New York City.[5]

That Willkie's name should ever have been seriously considered for the Republican Presidential nomination evidences the desperation to which the interventionists had been driven by the tide of American isolationist sentiment. Bellwether of the Willkie boom was the *New York Times,* but it found the going very hard indeed.

On November 29, 1939, the shrewd and realistic *Times* columnist, Arthur Krock, was ready to throw in the sponge. Willkie would make a strong candidate, said Krock, but to nominate him would take a miracle and "miracles don't happen any more." [6] Six months later the miracle was performed. The packed galleries which shouted "We want Willkie" got what they called for in the early morning of June 28, 1940. Never mind how they did it; it was done. "The most volatile ascension to party leadership in the history of American political parties" had been accomplished.[7]

Thus it had come to pass that at a crucial hour of American history, when the people of the United States were geared, conditioned and anxious for a great popular decision on the welfare state versus a return to American constitutional government, they were given a Hobson's choice between the two Presidential candidates, each of whom tried to outshout the other with loud promises to keep this country out of the European war. The irony was embittered by the

[5] *New York Times,* July 26, 1940, p. 11.
[6] *New York Times,* November 29, 1939.
[7] *The Republican Party and Wendell Willkie,* by Donad B. Johnson, (University of Illinois Press, Urbana, Ill.), pp. 44, 74 et seq.

subsequent realization that neither of these candidates had the slightest intention of keeping his pledged word.[8]

The interventionists had won the 1940 Presidential election when Willkie was nominated by the Republican Convention. They had known for a year that they must have it both ways in 1940 if they were ever again to have it at all. The risk investment which they had made in "the great and solemn referendum" of 1920 failed to pay off. That experi-

---

[8] "On October 30 . . . Willkie shouted that on the basis of Roosevelt's record of broken promises, his election would mean war within six months. Roosevelt was enroute to Boston the day that Willkie made this charge. By now Democratic leaders were more jittery than ever; the Gallup poll showed Willkie almost abreast of Roosevelt nationally, and ahead of him in New York and other key states. Each time his train stopped for rear-platform speeches on the way to Boston, messages came in . . . pleading with Roosevelt to answer Willkie's charges. The President, in fact, *had already compromised on the essential issue throughout the whole campaign by stressing his love for peace and neutrality and his record on defense, rather than expounding his crucial policy of aiding Britain even at the risk of war.* But as Roosevelt sat in a low-backed armed chair in his private car, Hopkins handed him a telegram from [National Democratic Chairman] Flynn insisting that he must reassure the people again about not sending Americans into foreign wars.

" 'But how often do they expect me to say that?' Roosevelt asked, 'It's in the Democratic platform and I've repeated it a hundred times.'

" 'Evidently' said Sherwood, 'You've got to say it again, and again and again.'

"That night in Boston, after a tumultuous reception, Roosevelt, . . . to the 'mothers and fathers of America' made the assurance that in years to come would be repeated mockingly by thousands of isolationist orators: "I have said this before, but I shall say it again and again and again: Your boys are not going to be sent into any foreign wars' " (Italics added.) *The Lion and the Fox,* supra, pp. 448-449.

"A month before the election (1940) the Democrats were denying that Wendell Willkie had ever been a Democrat; a month after the election, the Republicans were denying that he had ever been a Republican. . . . Alf Landon told a reporter: (1941) 'There is no essential difference between Mr. Willkie's position and Mr. Roosevelt's position, which is to go to war if necessary to help England win. If Mr. Willkie had revealed it before the Republican national convention, he would not have been nominated, and if Mr. Roosevelt had revealed it before the election he would not have been re-elected."

(*The Republican Party and Wendell Willkie,* supra, pp. 171-172)

ence convinced them that American voters must never again be given a clear chance for a real choice on the question of American independence. Henceforth, the Presidential candidates of both political parties must be Internationalists, Interventionists, or One Worlders—spell it as you please. The sure way to win the Presidency is to play for it without the risk of losing it. For the internationalists this formula has earned the best of all possible recommendations: it has worked.

5

"Me Too":
Roosevelt v. Dewey

☆☆☆☆☆

After the election of 1940 and its demolition of the anti-third-term tradition, Roosevelt made no secret of his intention to remain President of the United States as long as he lived. It was unnecessary now to be coy about a "draft" in the 1944 Democratic Convention. The only question left unanswered by Convention time was his final choice of a running mate.

After their party's defeat in 1940, disillusioned Republicans made haste to free themselves from Willkie's "leadership." Their work was cut out for them by Willkie himself when he publicly disdained his 1940 "campaign oratory" while testifying before a Congressional committee in support of Roosevelt's foreign policies.[1] But the 1940 standard-bearer did not give up his hopes for a second G.O.P. nomination in 1944. Officially, the Republican party had "closed ranks" behind the President in "an irresistible effort to win the war," but Willkie wanted the party to go further and resolve im-

[1] "In a speech on the floor of the House of Representatives, [November 6, 1941] Republican Representative Dewey Short of Missouri attacked Willkie violently as a 'belligerent, bombastic, bombinating, blow-hard, who couldn't be elected dog-catcher.' Short urged the House Republican Conference to repudiate Willkie." *New York Times,* February 12, 1941.

mediately in favor of a permanent international organization after victory was achieved.

In August, 1942, he left on a trip around the world as the personal representative of President Roosevelt, and subsequently wrote a well promoted "best seller" account of his journey under the significant title, *One World*.

Willkie's trip took him out of the country during the 1942 "off-year" Congressional campaign in which the Republicans gained 44 House seats and nine new members of the Senate. The Democratic delegation in Congress thus sank to the lowest point that it had reached since FDR was first inaugurated.

Conservatives were convinced that Willkie's absence had much to do with these Republican successes and Thomas E. Dewey's election as governor of New York immediately put him on top of the list of prospects for the 1944 Republican Presidential nomination. G.O.P. leaders saw in the encouraging Republican gains a sure sign that the New Deal had run its political course and that an orthodox Republican candidate, pledging a return to "normalcy" and "Americanism" would surely win the Presidency in 1944. However reluctantly, "liberal" commentators seemed to agree with this prognosis.[2]

But Wendell Willkie was undaunted. He contemptuously dismissed his Republican detractors as mouthpieces of reaction and isolationism. Ardently, he continued to believe with the *New York Times* editorialist:

"On the record he has made, on the merits of the causes he has led and so long as he goes straight ahead on the path which he has chosen, Wendell Willkie is head and shoulders above any

[2] For example, Walter Lippmann wrote: "The appointed time for a political change has arrived." *Time Magazine*, Nov. 15, 1943, p. 20.

other man in his right and title to that [1944 Republican] nomination." [3]

Confident that he had sold himself to the "grass roots"
of popular opinion, Willkie prepared to enter all 1944 state
Presidential primaries. In this hunt for Convention delegates, he made a vigorous campaign in and throughout the
State of Wisconsin where he preached "liberalism" and "internationalism" while he berated the Republican "bosses"
for their outdated conservatism.

But the voters were not impressed. When the Wisconsin
returns were tabulated, Willkie failed to elect a single delegate. On the other hand, Dewey, represented by a proxy
candidate whom Willkie described as "active in organizations such as America First (and) opposed to the beliefs
which I entertain," won seventeen of the state's 24 delegates.[4]

Immediately after this humiliating defeat, Willkie publicly withdrew his name from further consideration for the
1944 nomination. Conservative Republicans received the
news of Willkie's withdrawal with undisguised relief and
satisfaction. Commented the *Chicago Tribune:*

"His (Willkie's) power to harm the Republic by denying its voters
a choice of policies, has by his own confession ended."

The *Tribune's* conclusion was premature. Willkie had
withdrawn from the Presidential race but he did not thereby
end his efforts to press his liberal internationalist views upon
the Republican Party. This he had done and this he continued to do in a sustained stream of public speech and writing,
right up to the day of his sudden death on October 8, 1944.

3 *New York Times,* Oct. 16, 1943, p. 16
4 Of the remaining Wisconsin delegates elected, four were pledged to Harold
Stassen and three to General Douglas MacArthur.

Willkie had refrained from endorsing Thomas E. Dewey who had won the 1944 Republican nomination that Willkie had coveted and he was threatening a new political alignment with Roosevelt when he was stricken and taken to the hospital in September.[5]

As a matter of fact, Willkie had a low opinion of both Roosevelt and Dewey. He admitted privately that he was using his "neutrality" in the 1944 campaign deliberately as a lever to force Dewey into a public endorsement of his (Willkie's) policies.[6] Thus, in spite of the *Chicago Tribune's* hopeful conclusion, Willkie's "power to harm the Republic by denying its voters a choice of policies" did not end with the results of the Wisconsin primary in April, 1944. Willkie was using that power effectively when he died, and its impact was decisive in the closing weeks of the 1944 campaign.

In what could have been his home-stretch run to victory, Dewey forgot the popular forces that had repudiated Willkie-ism in the primaries and in the 1944 Republican convention. He side-stepped a confrontation with the sick and tired Roosevelt record and promised to continue the New Deal, but with more vigor, energy and orderliness.

[5] *Willkie*, by Joseph Barnes, (Simon and Schuster, New York, 1950) pp. 375-378.

[6] On August 25, the *New York Times* carried an article by Arthur Krock which praised Willkie's independent attitude. Willkie thanked Krock in a letter. He wrote:

"I happen to think of both Mr. Roosevelt and of Mr. Dewey as what I call pragmatic politicians. . . . I am greatly interested in creating a body of public opinion which will force either or both of them to go in the direction in which I believe they should. In other words, I believe that either one of them can be classified under either of those general terms, internationalist or isolationist. When it became politically expedient, Franklin D. Roosevelt repudiated the League of Nations. When it became politically expedient Thomas E. Dewey attacked the lease-lend bill. Likewise, both of them have made strong statements in favor of international cooperation. In the foreign field, I want to do what I can to force them in the latter direction."

(Quoted in *Willkie*, supra, p. 382.)

When Roosevelt taunted Dewey's new "me-too" Republicanism, the New York governor tried to "clarify" his position, but it was too late. The shade of Wendell Willkie had prevailed and once again the conservative voter lost his chance for a choice of policies.

Dewey did not lose the 1944 election single-handed. The "Old Maestro" in the White House had planned his fourth term campaign very carefully on the assumption that his Republican opposition in 1944 would be as strong and relentless as it might well have been, and as Roosevelt's advisors confidently expected that it would be. The President's formula for a fourth term was time-tested and relatively simple.

He planned to hold the southern states as firmly as he had always held them by the dispensation of plenty of job-making patronage. Under Roosevelt the "civil rights" issue was never permitted to boil over into a "Dixiecrat" revolt as it did under Truman in 1948. The President knew that in 1944 he would have the traditional 145 southern electoral votes safely in the bag. From there he could move on to New York State and add its big block of 47 electoral votes to his column for a total of 192. Momentum and political luck could be counted upon to give him the additional votes needed for victory, but for the success of the "formula," New York was indispensable.

In Presidential elections "upstate New York" could generally be relied upon to give Republican candidates a popular majority of 500,000. Thus to win the state's 47 electoral votes, Roosevelt would need a popular majority in New York City which would exceed a half-million. To obtain this insurance of a New York State victory, and the retention of the Presidency, it was necessary, of course, to get the complete enthusiastic support of the New York City Democratic organization, but that by itself was not enough.

The American Labor party had qualified for a place on the New York ballot in 1936, and polled nearly 275,000 votes in the November election of that year.[7] In 1936, Roosevelt had been chosen as the Presidential nominee of this new party which named the same slate of Presidential electors that had been put up by the Democrats. It is significant, too, that in 1936, the Communist party was on the ballot in New York and polled 36,609 votes for its Presidential candidate, Earl Browder. In New York State as elsewhere, Roosevelt's 1936 victory was of landslide proportions, and he did not need his American Labor party votes in order to carry his home state. But two years later the 1938 Congressional elections convinced the President that he was in for tough political sledding in 1940. He realized then that his "formula" would have to be played for all it was worth if he were to hold his lease on the White House in 1940. This conviction made it necessary for him to buy the support of the New York American Labor party at its asking price.

The Communist party had lost its place on the New York ballot because it polled too few votes in the governor's race of 1936, and by 1938 the Communists had come over to the American Labor party en masse. Immediately, they proceeded to take over that party's machinery in certain important areas of New York City. By using the 36,000 votes they had cast in 1936, the Communists were in a position to control the American Labor party and by controlling the American Labor party, they were in a position to control the Presidency of the United States.

Sidney Hillman, a co-proprietor of the American Labor party, with David Dubinsky, welcomed the Red recruits with

[7] Sidney Hillman and David Dubinsky, whose Amalgamated Clothing Workers Union and Ladies Garment Workers Union, respectively, had been saved by N.R.A., formed the American Labor Party to enable New Yorkers to vote for Roosevelt and still remain independent of the Democrats. *The Future of American Politics*, by Samuel Lubell, (Harper & Brothers, New York), p. 48.

open arms in spite of the fact that Dubinsky was disturbed by the Communist invasion. However, from 1938 to 1944, it was the Communist party who called the important shots for the American Labor Party in New York City and it was with them that President Roosevelt was forced to deal in order to insure the support of the American Labor party in the 1940 and the 1944 elections.[8]

8 Earl Browder was the Kremlin's top man in the United States during Franklin Roosevelt's Presidential administrations. F.D.R.'s rapport with Browder is an indication of the close liaison which the Communists had established with the White House on the basis of their crucial voting strength in New York City.

In January, 1940, Browder was convicted of passport fraud and was taken to Atlanta penitentiary on March 21, 1941, to begin serving a four-year term. At his trial, the government proved that Browder obtained a passport in 1921 in the name of Nicholas Dozenberg to visit Soviet Russia. He obtained another as George Morris in 1927 to do espionage work in China, and another under the name of Albert Henry Richards in 1931 to continue his spying activities in China. Later he obtained a legitimate pasport while swearing that he had never obtained a passport before. (*New York Herald Tribune,* March 17, 1942.) Browder's trial was forced, in effect, when he admitted before the Dies Committee in 1938 that he had resorted to fraudulent passports.

Agitation for the release of Browder began immediately, and "Free Browder" committees sprang up across the country. One of the functionaries selected by the Communists to lead the Free Browder campaign was Miss Josephine Truslow Adams, a descendant of Presidents John Adams and John Quincy Adams, who was an art teacher at Swarthmore College. On May 16, 1942, President Roosevelt freed Browder from the federal penitentiary by an Executive Order declaring that the release would "have a tendency to promote national unity and allay any feeling which may exist in some minds that the unusually long sentence was by way of penalty imposed upon him (Browder) because of his *political* views". (Italics added) (*New York Times,* May 17, 1942)

With Browder free, Miss Adams became the Communist Party's intermediary between Browder and the White House. The story of her services was not made public until 1957:

"A sensational and documented tale of a close World War II link between the late President Roosevelt and Earl Browder, former chief of the U.S. Communist Party, was unfolded today by the Senate Internal Security subcommittee. The subcommittee made public excerpts from testimony taken secretly in January from Josephine Truslow Adams, 57, a painter and art

When Hillman had repeatedly refused to expel the Communists, Dubinsky pulled his Ladies Garment Workers Union out of the American Labor party in 1944 and formed the Liberal party.

---

teacher who once lived at 225 E. 17th St., New York. Miss Adams, a descendant of Presidents John Adams and John Quincy Adams, detailed to the committee how she served as a go-between for F.D.R. and Browder, carrying dispatches, cables and a free flow of advice on political matters.

"Committee counsel Robert Morris announced that he had been authorized by Browder to confirm completely the account given by Miss Adams. The witness told of exchanges of advice and information between Browder and F.D.R. over the Tehran and Yalta conferences. Miss Adams testified that in addition to '38 or 40' personal visits to Roosevelt either at the White House or at his Hyde Park, N.Y., estate, where she spent the night a couple of times, she corresponded almost constantly with the President. Much of the time, she swore, she sent her letters through Mrs. Eleanor Roosevelt.

"The Adams testimony was backed solidly by Frank S. Meyer, a Woodstock, N.Y., writer and reformed Communist. Meyer said he had many long talks with Miss Adams about her activities at the White House and the relationship between Browder and F.D.R. He testified that Browder was using all means to influence the President's decisions. Miss Adams testified that Browder received secret military information from Red China and she personally carried one of the documents to the White House. Roosevelt did not want China to go Communist, she said, but he had little faith in the Nationalist government. (Browder, in a TV interview in New York last night, denied Miss Adams was a 'courier,' but a 'friend of mine and a friend of the President.' She reported his views on national issues to the President, Browder said, and she told Browder what the President's comments were.) Miss Adams previously had denied charges she served as Browder's White House courier. In December, 1953, she insisted she was an 'obscure and humble artist . . . not a mysterious cloak and dagger figure.'" (*New York Daily News*, February 27, 1957.)

Some indication of what Browder was telling the President through Miss Adams can be gathered from the following newspaper report of two speeches Browder made in September, 1943, in Chicago and in Gary, Indiana:

"When the President commuted the Federal prison sentence of Earl Browder on May 16, 1942, he gave as one of his reasons that the release of Stalin's henchman in this country would 'have a tendency to promote national unity.' Browder, who had served one year and two months of a four-year sentence for perjury and passport fraud, now has finally fulfilled the President's expectations. Nothing could have better served to unite the American people in their understanding and loathing of Communism—both Russian and do-

Without the assistance of American Labor party votes, Roosevelt would have lost New York State to Willkie in 1940 by 192,978 votes. If the American Labor party *or* Dubinsky's new Liberal party had failed to support Roosevelt in 1944, Dewey would have carried New York. As the Demo-

---

mestic—than the two speeches on Soviet policy which Browder has just delivered in Chicago and in Gary, Ind. The General Secretary of the Communist Party of the United States gave official substantiation to some bald facts about Soviet Russia and the dictatorship of Josef Stalin:

"1. Russia expects and demands all-out aid from Britain and the United States, but it is an 'illusion' for U.S. to expect that Russia 'will be able or willing to also undertake the burden of the military struggle against Japan. All this chatter about the Soviet's giving us bombing bases in Siberia is harmful nonsense.'

"2. Russia, for her own political reasons (which means the political reasons of Stalin, the absolute autocrat of the Soviet) will accept no 'second front' against Germany except the one of her own definition—a direct invasion through France at a cost of millions of Allied lives.

"3. Russia serves notice on Britain and the United States that they will be excluded from the reconstruction of Europe and Asia unless they extend 'major military aid,' which again in the Browder-Stalin definition, means nothing but a 'second front' in France.

"Browder's record as a subservient lackey of Stalin's is too long and lurid for his statements to be taken as his own personal views. He speaks for Stalin, as he has always spoken for Stalin. He has never deviated from the Communist line as it was laid down by Stalin. Ben Gitlow, expelled former head of the Communist Party here, testifying before the Dies Committee in 1939, gave the following description of Browder, the accuracy of which has been supported by subsequent events: 'Browder is Stalin's pet boy. He was personally named by Stalin, and several years ago when an effort was made to remove Browder, Stalin himself stepped in and stopped it. Moscow pays the bills and Moscow bosses the party.' When Hitler and Stalin joined hands in 1939, to loose war upon the world, it was Browder who was the chief American defender of the so-called Ten-Year Non-Aggression Pact. He opposed aid to Britain, opposed the Selective Service Act (he was himself a convicted draft dodger in World War I), and charged President Roosevelt, economic royalists and Wall Street with leading the U.S. into war. But he achieved a quick, if graceless, flipflop when Hitler launched the attack against Russia. The war that had been an 'imperialist war' became a 'peoples' war.' Nobody has cried 'second front' louder or oftener or with more anguish than the leader of the

cratic candidate in that election, Roosevelt received 2,478,-598 votes to Dewey's 2,987,647. In the same election, as the candidate of the American Labor party, Roosevelt received 496,405 New York votes, and as the Liberal party's candidate, he polled 329,325.[9] Thus the American Labor party alone in 1940, and either the American Labor party or the Liberal party in 1944, could have taken New York State

---

despicable group who call themselves 'American Communists,' and who did their level best to sabotage U.S. defense when Hitler and Stalin were pals. And now it is the same Browder, an American only by birth, a revolutionary who has openly advocated the destruction of our form of government, the servant and mouthpiece of Josef Stalin, who charges us with 'moral weakness' because our military leaders have wisely decided to follow their own judgment in the strategy of the war. As we said at the start, however, Browder has made good and done us a service even if unwittingly. He has given official clarification to Russian policy and intentions. He has shown up the 'American' Communist Party for what it is, despite the ostensible dissolution of the Commintern—still the same old subversive intruder, still working for Russia, still working against the United States. The warning is fair. It should be healthful. It should end some of our happy, wishful thinking. It should shock us out of the world of political make-believe. It should enable us to go ahead with our eyes wide open to such realities as Comrade Browder obligingly emphasized." (*New York Daily Mirror*, September 29, 1943.)

Earl Browder married Russian born Raissa Berkman in Moscow in 1926 and she came to the United States with him in 1926 (*New York Times*, 1955). In 1940 (during the Hitler-Stalin pact) deportation proceedings were brought against Mrs. Browder in the form of a warrant charging illegal entry into the United States. "However, she was allowed to re-enter the country legally from Canada after Mrs. Eleanor Roosevelt reportedly intervened." (*New York Daily News*, February 26, 1953.)

On April 12, 1946, exactly one year after the death of President Roosevelt, Mrs. Browder filed a petition for naturalization which was denied. October 14, 1949, Mr. and Mrs. Browder were examined under oath and both denied that she was or had ever been a member of the Communist party. Subsequently, both were indicted on charges that this denial of Communist party membership was false. After a long series of delays the Browders were jailed in 1952 and then released on bail. Mrs. Browder died in 1954. Earl Browder has never been tried on this charge of perjury.

9 *World Almanac*, 1962, p. 436.

from Roosevelt by nominating a Presidential candidate other than F.D.R. As it turned out, Roosevelt would have won both of those Presidential elections without the electoral votes of New York, but no Democratic candidate for President with the political competence of Franklin D. Roosevelt would have made his plans on that expectation.[10]

The American Labor party disintegrated and disappeared into the Liberal party after the death of Sidney Hillman on July 10, 1946.

As we have seen, Roosevelt's Presidential campaigns were always conducted on the assumption that the electoral votes of New York were essential. Since victory in New York was thus a necessary prerequisite to the success of his plans, Roosevelt was never under any illusions about the indispensability of the Hillman-Dubinsky combination in New York City. Although he did not attend the Democratic nominating convention of 1944, the President was in close touch by telephone with the party directorate in Chicago. The only real decision to be made by the convention was the choice of Roosevelt's running mate. The President was "cagey" in his suggestions of eligibles. A number of his ambitious associates were angling for his endorsement. Roosevelt's final instruction on the vice-presidential candidacy was "to clear it with Sidney (Hillman)." In Roosevelt's calculations, a vice-presidential candidate without Hillman's blessing would mean the loss of New York and the election. It was Sidney Hillman, therefore, who told Harry S. Truman

[10] New York had 47 electoral votes in 1940 and 1944. The number was later reduced to 45.

In 1960 Kennedy would have lost New York *and the election* to Nixon without the votes of the Liberal party. The New York popular vote in 1960 was:

Kennedy: Democratic candidate —3,423,909
Nixon: Republican candidate —3,446,419
Kennedy: Liberal candidate   — 406,176

that he, the Senator from Missouri, had been chosen.[11] The means were sordid, but for F.D.R., the big end justified them completely.

[11] On Tuesday, July 18, two days after his arrival in Chicago, Hillman, who was stopping at the Ambassador East Hotel, had Senator Truman as a guest for breakfast. . . . Mr. Truman . . . asked Hillman whether he could depend upon his support for Byrnes. "No," said Hillman, . . . "we are for Wallace, but we might accept two other men. . . . I am looking at our first choice now."

Sidney Hillman, by Matthew Josephson (Doubleday and Company, New York, 1952), p. 621 et seq.

6

"Me Two":
Truman v. Dewey

☆☆☆☆☆

The makeshift political roof that sheltered Franklin D. Roosevelt through four Presidential elections fell in upon Harry S. Truman in 1948. By and large his succession to the Presidency in 1945 gave the American people a welcome change of political pace. Truman began his administration of the government with modesty and moderation. He made no formal break with the New Deal tradition but neither did he make any move to push it into new frontiers. In 1945, the American people were tired of crusades at home and abroad. Like Calvin Coolidge, after World War I, Truman, in the first post World War II years, provided a political sedative that the American people were more than ready to accept.

In late 1947, the Gallup Poll favored the President to win re-election over either Taft or Dewey. On November 7, 1947, David Lawrence wrote that "the chances that the Republicans will win in 1948 are less than even . . . no matter whom the Republicans select as their candidate." Then came the great "nose dive" in the President's curve of popularity. His State of the Union Message to the Republican 80th Congress was a mixture of the cause and the effect of his fall from popular grace.

Truman delivered the message in person on January 7, just nine days after Henry Wallace had announced the formation of his new Progressive party which appealed for the support of the far-left New Dealers. As the President's address to Congress unfolded it became evident that he was frightened by the Wallace movement and had decided to anticipate its platform and to pre-empt its popular appeal. For the first time since he became President, Truman put on the mantle of the crusading New Dealer in a series of proposals for more social security, public housing, farm price supports, aid to education and higher minimum wages. Democratic Congressmen heard the speech in stony silence, and when the President left the rostrum Republicans were quick to blast the message unmercifully. Newspaper comment was uniformly critical, and by nightfall it was evident that the era of good feeling for Truman had ended.

In February the President's declining political prospects worsened with the report of the Civil Rights Committee which he had appointed in 1946. Its recommendations were drastic, and volleys of indignant protest reverberated throughout the Democratic South triggered by the outraged roars of southern senators, representatives and governors who threatened to bolt the Democratic party in the fall elections.

A movement developed to deprive Truman of the Democratic nomination and to name General Dwight D. Eisenhower to lead the ticket in 1948. Ironically, the Eisenhower suggestion was applauded as enthusiastically by the conservative, civil-rights-conscious Southerners as it was by the liberal Americans for Democratic Action led by James Roosevelt. The "Draft Ike" movement persisted until July 5, one week before the Democratic Convention met at Philadelphia. On that day Eisenhower announced that he would not "at this time" accept nomination for any political office. On the moot point as to whether Eisenhower was in fact a Democrat, the General said nothing. At this late hour, it was impossible for the President's opponents to regroup behind another candidate and so the Democrats were compelled to commit what H. L. Mencken called "Trumanocide."

Before the President was renominated, delegates from Mississippi and Alabama left the Convention in protest against the civil rights plank that was adopted in a bitter floor fight under the prodding of the A.D.A. One out of every four delegates present had voted for Senator Russell of Georgia for the Presidential nomination, and these dissenters spurned a plea to make Truman's nomination unanimous.

On July 17 a convention of anti-Truman States Rights Democrats met in Birmingham, Alabama, and nominated Governor Strom Thurmond of South Carolina for President and Governor Fielding L. Wright of Mississippi for Vice President. Two weeks later Henry Wallace and United States Senator Glenn Taylor of Idaho were named for President and Vice President respectively by the new Progressive party at a convention in Philadelphia.

Thus Truman went into the 1948 campaign with his party truncated, right and left. Facing what they regarded as certain defeat after 20 years of national dominance, organization Democrats were bitterly vilifying the President as a vain little man who chose to wreck his party rather than acknowledge his notorious incapabilities. In the late summer of 1948 Truman's political posture was truly pathetic. The incongruous blocks of Southerners, Socialists, Negroes, Communists, city bosses, intellectuals, labor leaders and internationalists that Franklin D. Roosevelt had held together through four Presidential elections were now scattered to the four political winds. Where could the beleaguered President look for

strength to defend his position? Truman did not look for de-
fenders. He took his cue from the famous message sent by
General Foch to Marshal Joffre during the first battle of the
Marne in August, 1914:

> My right has been rolled up;
> My left has been driven back;
> I have ordered a fullscale attack upon the center.

In this spirit Truman forgot his floundering flanks and
launched an all-out, unremitting attack upon the Republicans' strongest point—the record of the 80th Congress.

In the election of 1946 the Republican party had won a
majority of both Houses of Congress for the first time in 16
years. Never before had a legislative majority moved in more
quickly to take charge of the federal government in spite of
the shrill passionate protest of its President. Over Truman's
veto the 80th Congress passed the Taft-Hartley Act to soften
the power of labor union monopolies that had ruled pretty
much as they pleased since the first months of the New Deal.
Truman flayed this legislation as a "slave labor" law and
called down the maledictions of Heaven upon its authors.
(Nevertheless, none of the succeeding Democratic Con-
gresses has seriously sought to repeal the Taft-Hartley Act.)
In 1947, the new 80th Congress trimmed $20,000,000,000 out
of the previous year's budget total and wound up the year
with a $750,000 surplus.

Congressman Daniel A. Reed of New York, who was rank-
ing Republican member of the House Ways and Means
Committee at that time, subsequently described their accomplishment in this way:

"In the 80th Congress we balanced the budget for the first time
in 17 years. We cut taxes (for the first time since 1929) and as a

result, got more revenue. Instead of a twenty-billion dollar deficit we paid five billion dollars on the National Debt and had a surplus at the end of two years of eight billion dollars." [1]

For some strange reason Harry S. Truman concluded that this Republican record of tax cutting, budget balancing and debt reduction gave him the issue he needed to win his unpromising campaign for re-election. For an even stranger reason, the Republican high command seemed to agree with him. When Truman denounced the "do-nothing— Eighty-Worst" Congress at every whistle stop from coast to coast, Republican nominee, Thomas E. Dewey, simply ignored the loud little man who had already been so soundly defeated in the Gallup Poll. Jules Ables in his fascinating analysis of this phenomenal 1948 campaign says:

"Dewey explains that he did not defend the Eightieth Congress because 'I have never fought on a battleground of another's choosing in a campaign.' But it would appear that Dewey did not defend the Eightieth Congress because he felt in his own heart that Truman was right, that it (the Eightieth Congress) was a nest of reactionaries. Brownell [Dewey's campaign manager] and Bell [Dewey's chief ghost writer] admit as much. Dewey says, 'The issue was not the Eightieth Congress. It was the *liberal* platform adopted by the Republican Party." [2] (Italics added.)

This belief that Truman's "big lie" was the truth was shared by the chairman of the National Republican Committee, Hugh Scott, of Pennsylvania. When the returns showed that Truman had been re-elected, Scott told the assembled reporters, "partly in frustration, and partly also in hope" that the Republican defeat was "a good thing." "Those masto-

[1] *U.S. News and World Report*, June 19, 1953.
[2] *Out of the Jaws of Victory*, by Jules Abels (Henry Holt and Co.), p. 194.

dons (in the Eightieth Congress) wouldn't listen to me. They had to learn their lesson. Now maybe they'll go out and pass some good social legislation." [3]

The tragedy was that many of those Republican conservatives whom Scott regarded as "mastodons" had been crucified in their campaign for re-election to Congress because their party's Presidential candidate refused to refute Truman's false statements about their record. Dewey's attitude put these Congressmen in an impossible position politically. An outstanding casualty was Harold Knutson of Minnesota who had been a member of Congress since 1917 and who was chairman of the Ways and Means Committee of the House of Representatives in the 80th Congress. As the chief architect of the tax cutting, budget balancing and debt reducing record of the "do-nothing" Congress, Knutson was one of Truman's principal targets. He and others like him were defeated for re-election in 1948 because they were forced to run against their own party's candidate for President.

In Dewey's political perspective there were no conservative votes to be attracted to Republican support in 1948. He assumed that his task was to switch Democratic and independent liberals to the Republican side. North of the Mason-Dixon line, conservatives could choose between Wallace, Truman and Dewey. Millions of them chose to stay at home on election day or if they went to the polls, they voted for minor candidates and passed up the Presidential race.

Thus it was that Dewey, having learned nothing in his trial run against FDR in 1944, contrived against overwhelming odds to snatch a second defeat "out of the jaws of victory." Dewey's ironical achievement marked the third time in succession that the Conservative American's chance for a choice had been left at the post when the Presidential nominating

[3] Joseph Harsch, *The Christian Science Monitor*, Jan. 17, 1956.

conventions adjourned. Whatever else is to be said of him, political historians will have to admit that throughout his long travail, the Conservative American has managed to maintain a remarkably high boiling point.

7

The Texas Steal:
Taft v. Eisenhower

☆☆☆☆☆

After his 1948 defeat, Thomas E. Dewey's Presidential prospects were all behind him. He removed himself from further consideration for the high office in a firm public statement on October 15, 1950, in which he suggested that General Eisenhower be drafted to lead the G.O.P. in 1952 and promised to support such a move if it developed.

A month later in Ohio, Senator Robert A. Taft won re-election to the United States Senate by a margin of 437,000 votes. This was the greatest plurality ever given to an Ohio senator. Taft's total vote in what had been expected to be a light "off year" election was 1,642,537, or nearly 197,000 more votes than Dewey had received when he lost Ohio to Truman in the Presidential election of 1948. Union labor leaders had gone all out to beat Taft in 1950 for his sponsorship of the Taft-Hartley "slave labor" law. Their humiliating defeat demonstrated the extent of Dewey's miscalculation in 1948 when he refused to confront Truman on the record of the 80th Congress.

Taft emerged from his 1950 re-election as "Mr. Republican." At that time the designation was as popular as it was promising. Truman's second administration was skidding into a period of bitterness and frustration. The President's

United Nations "police action" in Korea was unpopular and unsuccessful. When General Douglas MacArthur insisted upon winning the war by bombing the Red Chinese sanctuary beyond the Yalu River in Manchuria, Truman removed him from his Korea command, and the distinguished military leader returned to this country to be greeted everywhere by cheering multitudes.[1] On April 19, 1951, MacArthur climaxed his triumphal homecoming with an address to Congress that was a classic exposition of his famous thesis that "In war there is no substitute for victory."

The Korean conflict went from bad to worse. Senator Joseph R. McCarthy's charges concerning Communists in the government were making headlines which were climaxed later by the dismissal of John Carter Vincent from the State Department, the indictment of Owen Lattimore and the conviction of the Communist spies, Julius and Ethel Rosenberg. Throughout the congressional session which began in 1951 the Truman Administration was pilloried with charges of influence peddling, tax frauds and "softness toward Communism." All this added up to "the mess in Washington" which was fast congealing into the big issue for the next Presidential campaign.

Throughout 1951 it was a foregone conclusion that the Republicans would win the Presidency in 1952. It seemed equally certain that the new President's name would be Robert A. Taft because there was no *Republican* in the country who could successfully challenge Taft's right to obtain the Republican nomination. Conservative Americans

---

1 "When MacArthur insisted that the added effort was needed to get victory, the General was summarily fired. The action was taken because, according to President Truman's description, MacArthur was 'unable to give his whole-hearted support to the policies of the United States government. . . .' His firing was explained as necessary to preserve the supremacy of the civilian over the military in government." *U.S. News and World Report*, Sept. 19, 1952, p. 14.

were jubilant. They were sure that in 1952 their long chance for a clear choice, which had been champing at the bit for sixteen years, would finally clear the starting gate and go on to give them a real run for their money in the Presidential sweepstakes. But at that point things began to happen.

In 1959, *U.S. News and World Report* published Taft's own play-by-play account of *how* he lost the Republication nomination in 1952.[2] This is a most important revelation. But it is even more important to know *why* Taft lost that nomination to a man who had no formal political affiliations, who had been boomed for the Democratic nomination in 1948, and who to this day has given no indication that he knew the real reason why he was then being chosen to derail "Mr. Republican's" victory train.

Any one of a dozen honest and reputable Republicans could have won the Presidential election in 1952. The Democrats had no record to run on and nobody who was able and anxious to do the running. It was precisely because the Democrats were doomed to certain defeat that Taft was deprived of his vested right to defeat them. The first ingredient in the stop-Taft formula was irony. The very same people who experienced no compunctions when they steered Willkie and Dewey into nominations that resulted in three successive Republican defeats suddenly became "victory conscious" as 1952 drew near. Their first pitch to the public was bland, even apologetic, to wit:

"Taft is a truly great person. He can get the Republican nomination for President and he undoubtedly deserves it, but of course he can't win the election."

In the bright light of Ohio's 1950 election returns such an unblinking conclusion lacked logic, but this "Madison Ave-

2 *U.S. News and World Report,* Dec. 7, 1959.

nue" line was not meant to be logical; it was purely psycho-logical. The logical arguments that the stop-Taft people developed against the Ohio senator in 1952 could not be used except amongst themselves. The logical major premise upon which their frantic effort was based was their common conviction that unless they could manage to prevent it, Taft certainly would be nominated *and* elected President in 1952. This definite prospect appalled them. Why?

It was not love for union labor nor devotion to the expensive domestic institutions of the New Deal that filled these people with a frenzied fear of Taft as President. The prospect of Taft's election frightened them because they knew that, as President, Taft would break their hold upon American foreign policy and turn that policy in the direction of American interests. Taft was continuing to stress his conviction that our capricious foreign policy must be restored to its proper confinement within the Constitution of the United States. He condemned the "Truman-Acheson-Marshall foreign policy" as a complete failure which perverted American interests and violated American principles.[3] To put it bluntly, Taft was for America first.

[3] In 1951 Taft's book *A Foreign Policy for America* was published (Doubleday and Company, New York). Its basic premise was clearly stated: "The ultimate purpose of our foreign policy must be to protect the liberty of the people of the United States. War should never be undertaken, or seriously risked, except to protect American liberty." In this book, Taft denied that the United States had any moral obligation or Constitutional right to try to raise the living standards of the world because "that is utterly beyond our capacity." . . . I think we can take the leadership in proclaiming the doctrines of liberty and justice and in impressing the world that only through liberty, law and justice, and not through Socialism or Communism, can the world hope to obtain the standards which we have obtained in the United States. Our leaders can at least stop apologizing for the American system. . . . The most alarming thing is that there seems to be so many responsible people in the country who follow the party line of the State Department with complete blindness . . . in spite of the fact that it has led us a long way toward disaster recently. . . . In doing so they blithely dismiss all in-

This was the reason why the stop-Taft people were determined to prevent his nomination by the Republican Convention, and, conversely, it was their reason why they used Eisenhower to achieve their purpose. But this was not a reason that would have appealed to the American people. Consequently, the stop-Taft cabal, using its limitless resources for such accomplishments, induced thousands of good Republican innocents to repeat: "Taft is wonderful but he can-

---

terest in the maintenance of popular government under the Constitution. They are obviously afraid of popular government, thinking that the people are too dumb to understand foreign policy. . . . The framers of the Constitution provided expressly that only Congress can do certain things." (pp. 11, 15, 17, 26.)

Taft had no patience with the "One Worlders": "The theory of an international state bearing the same relation to nations and their citizens as our federal government bears to the states appears to me to be fantastic, dangerous and impractical. . . . The difficulties of holding together such a Tower of Babel would be insuperable. . . . True freedom depends on local self-government and effective access of the people to their individual rights. . . . If we can once convince ourselves that we believe in freedom, then there are many things which we can do throughout the world to meet the threat of Communism. . . . I believe that an able and courageous leader could successfully work out a system *which would give the Soviet Government something to worry about behind the Iron Curtain.* . . . It seems to me perfectly clear that the President's power as Commander in Chief does not extend to the delegation of that power to a commander who is chosen by any other nation or any other group of nations. I think that it is perfectly clear that he cannot enter into an agreement of that kind to set up an international army without submitting the agreement to Congress. . . . But whether there is to be an American Army or an international army, I do not believe the President has the power without congressional approval to send troops to one country to defend it against a possible or probable attack by another country. Such action may *perhaps* be authorized by treaty but it has not been authorized either by the United Nations Charter or by the Atlantic Pact. . . . *If the President can carry out every recommendation of the Security Council or the General Assembly* (of the United Nations) *supported by the vote of the American representative whom he can direct, then he has almost unlimited power to do anything in the world . . . without the slightest voice* of Congress in the matter. If that could be the effect of an international treaty, we had better watch closely the approval of any such treaty in the future." Supra pp. 45, 119, 36. (Italics added.)

not win. We simply must not lose this long-awaited chance to turn the rascals out." The hypocrisy of those who coined this cliche was demonstrated by their proposed alternative, namely, Eisenhower. If they had been interested merely in a glamorous candidate to insure a November victory, they could have drafted General Douglas MacArthur who was a bona fide Republican and undoubtedly receptive. But the stop-Taft people knew that MacArthur's foreign policy would be just as American and therefore just as abhorrent as the Ohio senator's.

The job of displacing Taft as the Republican nominee proved to be Herculean. In spite of his military training and experience, Eisenhower had no stomach for political in-fighting and he played extremely hard-to-get. Paul G. Hoff-man went to Europe in 1951 with instructions to stay until he obtained the distinguished N.A.T.O. Commander's con-sent to accept the Republican nomination if it were offered to him. Hoffman could not swing the assignment and Sena-tor Henry Cabot Lodge flew to Paris in December to help the cause. Back in Washington on January 6, 1962, Lodge told a press conference that he had just had General Eisen-hower's personal answer to the big $64 question. "He is a Republican," said Lodge. "I invite you to check this in Paris," he added, "and I will not be repudiated." Senator Lodge explained that he had assured Governor Sherman Adams of New Hampshire that General Eisenhower would be entered as a candidate for the Presidency on the Republi-can ticket in the New Hampshire primary and that the General would be in the race to the finish.

The next day, January 7, from Supreme Headquarters of the Allied Powers in Europe came an announcement by General Eisenhower. He acknowledged that Lodge was right in labeling him a Republican and added: "He (Senator

Lodge) was correct also in stating that I would not seek nomination to political office (sic) . . . and I shall not participate in the pre-Convention activities of others who may have such intention with respect to me. . . . *In the absence, however, of a clear-cut call to political duty, I shall continue to devote my full attention to the task to which I am assigned.*" (Italics added.) If Eisenhower really meant what he said on January 7, 1952, he subsequently changed his mind —or had it changed for him.

In the immediately succeeding months "the clear-cut call to political duty" was muted to inaudibility by the raucous clamor of bruising primary battles. In March, even the Gallop Poll of Republicans gave Taft the lead, and the latter's victories in Wisconsin and Nebraska on April 1 sent Lodge scurrying back to Paris where General Eisenhower let it be known that he would be home "in time to take a personal hand in the campaign." He notified the Secretary of Defense that "as of now (April 2) I consider that the specific purposes for which I was recalled to duty have been largely accomplished," and the White House announced that he would be relieved of his N.A.T.O. command on June 1.

Eisenhower resigned from the Army on June 2 and hastened to Kansas for his first political speech on June 3. Hearing only clamor, he had decided to sound the "clear-cut call" himself. By Convention time (July 7) the call was still unclear, but by then the Eisenhower managers had forgotten all about "the call." In desperation they had to seize upon the "Texas Steal." They were alleging that Robert A. Taft was a thief. Here is the account from a "progressive" Republican historian who gratefully acknowledges help from Walter Lippman, James Reston, Joseph and Stewart Alsop, Roscoe Drummond, "and many others." He is definitely not "pro-Taft."

"Eager for an issue that would halt or at least slow down the momentum of the Taft campaign, Eisenhower strategists prepared to make the most out of the promised conflict over the seating of the Texas delegates. Backers of Robert Taft in Texas, said Ike on June 21 at Dallas, were guilty of 'a betrayal of the whole Republican Party and its principles' when they 'deliberately and ruthlessly disenfranchised the majorities that voted for another candidate at the precinct and county conventions. . . .' The Texas 'steal' as press, radio and television took up the chant, was a story that spread throughout the nation." [4]

Eisenhower's managers made the most of this "story." *Thou shalt not steal* became their official printed slogan at the Convention Hall and black bandit "stop thief" masks were passed out in the thronged Chicago hotel lobbies. This was the fat they finally threw into the fire that had refused to respond to the big forced draft. By the light of this flare, the stop-Taft forces went on to win the nomination for their glamorous draftee.

In his own explanation of his defeat Taft completely exonerated any particular person or any single piece of strategy from responsibility. It is evident now that the Ohio Senator defeated himself by underestimating the desperate determination of the forces working against him. Taft was overconfident. His friends were in charge of the Party and they were expected to manage the Convention. The 1952 platform was written in confident anticipation of Taft's nomination.[5] Guilelessly, the Taft forces fell into the trap that had

---

[4] *The Republicans, A History of their Party,* by Malcolm Moos (Random House, Inc., New York, 1956), p. 468.

[5] The Republican Platform of 1952 contained these "planks":

We shall eliminate from the State Department and from every federal office, all, wherever they may be found, who share responsibility for the needless predicaments and perils in which we find ourselves. *We shall* also sever from the public payroll the hordes of loafers, incompetents and unnecessary employees who clutter the administration of our foreign affairs. The confusions,

been set for them. The Senator's managers actually believed that Taft was being opposed because his enemies were convinced that he could not win the election. And consequently they kept insisting that he could win it, which did nothing except to dignify his opponents with the presumption of

---

overlappings, and extravagance of our agencies abroad hold us up to the ridicule of peoples whose friendship we seek. . . .

The Government of the United States, under Republican leadership, will repudiate all commitments contained in secret understandings such as those of Yalta which aid Communist enslavements. It will be made clear, on the highest authority of the President and the Congress, that United States policy, as one of its peaceful purposes, looks happily forward to the genuine independence of those captive peoples.

We shall make liberty into a beacon light of hope again that will penetrate the dark places. That program will give the Voice of America a real function. It will mark the end of the negative, futile and *immoral policy of 'containment'* which abandons countless human beings to a despotism and godless terrorism, which in turn enables the rulers to forge the captives into a weapon for our destruction. . . .

We shall see to it that no treaty or agreement with other countries deprives our citizens of the rights guaranteed them by the Federal Constitution.

We shall always measure our foreign commitments so that they can be borne without endangering the economic health or sound finances of the United States. Stalin said that 'the moment for the decisive blow' would be when the free nations were isolated and were in a state of 'practical bankruptcy.' We shall not allow ourselves to be isolated and economically strangled, and we shall not let ourselves go bankrupt.

Sums available by this test, if competently used, will be more effective than vastly larger sums incompetently spent for vague and endless purposes. We shall not try to buy good will. We shall earn it by sound, constructive self-respecting policies and actions. . . .

The policies we espouse will revive the contagious, liberating influences which are inherent in freedom. They will inevitably set up strains and stresses within the captive world which will make the rulers impotent to continue in their monstrous ways and mark the beginning of their end. . . .

COMMUNISM. By the Administration's appeasement of Communism at home and abroad it has permitted Communists and their fellow travelers to serve in many key agencies and to infiltrate our American life. When such infiltrations became notorious through the revelations of Republicans in Congress, the Executive Department stubbornly refused to deal with it openly and vigorously. It raised the false cry of 'red herring' and took other measures to block and discredit investigations. It denied files and information to

good faith. While Taft was offering to give away a portion of his duly elected delegates from Texas in order to show fairness and to avoid party discord, Governor Dewey was holding his New York delegation in Star Chamber sessions, bludgeoning and browbeating a score of openly committed

---

Congress. It set up boards of its own to keep information secret and to deal lightly with security risks and persons of doubtful loyalty. It only undertook prosecution of the most notorious Communists after public opinion forced action. . . .

A Republican President will appoint only persons of unquestioned loyalty. We will overhaul loyalty and security programs. In achieving these purposes a Republican President will cooperate with Congress. We pledge close coordination of our intelligence services for protecting our security. We pledge fair but vigorous enforcement of laws to safeguard our country from subversion and disloyalty. By such policies we will keep the country secure and restore the confidence of the American people in the integrity of our Government. . . .

TAXATION AND MONETARY POLICY. Only with a sound economy can we properly carry out both the domestic and foreign policies which we advocate. The wanton extravagance and inflationary policies of the Administration in power have cut the value of the dollar in half and imposed the most confiscatory taxes in our history. These policies have made the effective control of Government expenditures impossible. If this Administration is left in power, it will further cheapen the dollar, rob the wage earner, impoverish the farmer and reduce the true value of the savings, pensions, insurance, and investments of millions of our people. Further inflation must be and can be prevented. Sound tax and monetary policies are essential to this end. . . .

To the Working Man:—
    The right to quit his job at any time.
    The right to take part in legal union activities.
    The right to remain in his union so long as he pays his dues.
    The right to protection against unfair practices by either employer or union officials.
    The right to political activity of his own choice and freedom to contribute thereto.
    The right to a job without first joining a union.
    The right to a secret ballot in any election concerned with his livelihood.
    The right to protection from personal financial responsibility in damage cases against his union.

Taft delegates into the Eisenhower column. This had gone on in New York for weeks before the Convention and it continued in Chicago right up to the time of the roll call. Only two New Yorkers finally withstood the official pressure, which visibly annoyed their busy little Governor who had promised the Eisenhower forces a solid delegation.

Eisenhower's nomination left the Republicans riven in rancor and bitterness. One delegate declared as he left Chi-

---

To the Labor Unions:—

The right to establish 'union shop' contracts by agreement with management.

The right to strike.

The right to free collective bargaining.

The right to protection from rival unions during the life of union contracts.

The right to assurance from employers that they will bargain only with certified unions as a protection against unfair labor practices.

We urge the adoption of such amendments to the Taft-Hartley Act as time and experience show to be desirable, and which further protect the rights of labor, management and the public.

We condemn the President's seizure of plants and industries to force the settlement of labor disputes by claims of inherent Constitutional powers. . . . We shall make a thorough study of universal pay-as-we-go pension plans.

REPUBLICAN 80TH CONGRESS:

The Republican Party does not rest its case upon promises alone. We have a record of performance which was grossly defamed by the Party in power. *The Republican 80th Congress launched the program to stop Communism;* unified the armed services; authorized a 70-group Air Force which the President blocked; enacted a national service law; balanced the budget; accumulated an eight-billion-dollar surplus; reduced taxes, with 70 per cent of the tax savings to those with incomes under $5,000; freed 7,400,000 wage earners in the lower brackets from having to pay any further income tax at all; allowed married couples to divide their incomes for tax purposes, and granted an additional $600 exemption to those over 65 years of age and to the blind; enacted the Taft-Hartley law for equitable labor-management relations; passed the first long-range agriculture program; increased social security benefits; and carried out every single pledge they made to the voters in the 1946 election.

cago that those who had leaped for the Eisenhower band-
wagon had actually jumped upon a hearse heading for the
grave of the Republican party.[6]

The 1952 frustration was not a new experience for rank
and file conservatives but its impact upon those Republicans
who had so confidently fronted the Taft organization left
many of these people in a state of shock. There were rum-
bles of an independent party that would nominate General
MacArthur for President. After his perfunctory handshake
with Eisenhower immediately following the latter's nomination, Taft left for Canada and said nothing further for
publication. Later in July, the Democrats nominated Governor Adlai Stevenson of Illinois. Thus having once again insured itself against defeat in the election, the internationalist
cabal decorously backed out of the political limelight and
graciously allowed the American people to believe that
they were about to select a President of the United States.

Immediately after the Conventions, the outcome of the
November election, which had so long loomed as a sure victory for the Republican party, was clouded in doubt and
speculation. Fearing a sit-out by conservatives, Republican
leaders began to quote their platform, most of which was a
legacy from Taft. Over the vehement objections of party liberals, Senator Joseph R. McCarthy was hustled onto the
hustings where he needled Stevenson about his court deposi-
tion in support of Alger Hiss, and underscored the Republican platform promise to protect the country from Communist subversion by the co-operation of the President with
congressional investigations.

On July 17, Eisenhower sent Taft a telegram requesting his
assistance in the campaign, but the Ohio Senator let it be
known that he would have nothing to say about the coming
election until he had a meeting and an understanding with

6 *The Republicans, A History of Their Party,* by Malcolm Moos, supra, p. 482.

General Eisenhower. Meanwhile the Eisenhower band-wagon slowed down to an uninspiring walk. In late August the pro-Eisenhower Scripps-Howard newspapers lashed out at the Republican campaign in a front page editorial which stated that Ike was "running like a dry creek." Three weeks later the long-awaited Taft-Eisenhower confrontation took place on September 12 at the General's Morningside Drive residence in New York. Taft brought to the meeting a long statement setting forth his understanding of Eisenhower's attitude on leading issues.[7] After conferring privately for three

---

[7] "Meeting with reporters and radio commentators following the conference, Senator Taft said that General Eisenhower and he were in accord on domestic issues and that their differences of opinion on foreign policy was one of degree rather than purpose. . . . Taft said: 'I have never changed my intention expressed in Chicago, but, of course, I have not intended to abandon in any way the principles I have fought for for the past fourteen years or abandon those countless friends who supported me in the pre-convention campaign. I have felt, therefore, that I could be far more effective in the campaign if I could state to the people after talking with General Eisenhower my definite conviction regarding the character of his administration when he is elected and the principles by which it will be guided.

" 'A good many of my friends have been concerned because so many of his editorial and columnist supporters and other individuals, who have always heretofore taken the New Deal line, have been urging him to repudiate the Republican platform, approve the New Deal policies and purge everyone who has fought hard for Republican principles against Truman and Acheson and the rest of the left-wingers. I have felt confident that General Eisenhower had no such intentions. The expression of such a confidence can be far more effective after a personal talk with him.

" 'As I see it, there is and has been one great fundamental issue between the Republican Party and the New Deal or Fair Deal or Stevenson Deal. It is the issue of liberty against the creeping Socialization in every domestic field. Liberty was the foundation of our government, the reason for our growth, the basis of our happiness, and the hope of the future. The greatest threat to liberty today is internal, from the constant growth of big government, through the constantly increasing power and expanding of the federal government. The price of continued liberty, including a free economic system, is the reduction of federal spending and taxes, the repudiation of arbitrary powers in the Executive, claimed to be derived from Heaven, and the stand

hours, Taft and Eisenhower met the press together and the General expressed his "full agreement" with the Taft manifesto. This brought forth a blast of protest from pinks and liberals who were shocked at Eisenhower's acceptance of Taft's "right-wing ultimatum." But the "Taft-Eisenhower

---

against statutory extension of power by the creation and extension of federal bureaus. . . .

" 'Today we are up against the guns. Government is taking one-third of our peoples' income and thereby one-third of their freedom. I wished to be sure that the new administration will be inspired with the philosophy of extending liberty before I entered into an extensive speaking campaign.

" 'After a satisfactory discussion with General Eisenhower this morning for two hours, I am satisfied that this is his philosophy. I am convinced that he will carry out the pledges of the Republican platform which expresses that philosophy adopted unanimously by Republican representatives from all parts of the country under the leadership of Senator Millikin. I recognize, of course, that the platform is not specific in every regard and that the candidate must have the right to develop the details of the program within the general spirit of the platform. . . .

" 'General Eisenhower has also told me that he believes strongly in our system of constitutional limitations on government power, that he abhors the left-wing theory that the Executive has unlimited powers such as Mr. Truman claimed that he could seize steel mills and usurp other powers generally without constitutional authority.

" 'General Eisenhower has also told me that he believes in the basic principles of the Taft-Hartley law, its protection of the freedom of the people and union members themselves against the arbitrary use of power by big business or big labor and is opposed to its repeal. . . .

" 'General Eisenhower agreed that the proper role of the federal government is one of advice, research and assistance to the states, the local communities and the people. . . .

" 'I am completely satisfied that General Eisenhower will give this country an administration inspired by Republican principles of continued and expanding liberty for all as against the continued growth of New Deal socialism which we would suffer under Governor Stevenson, representative of the left-wingers, if not a left-winger himself.

" 'I urge all Americans and particularly those who have confidence in my judgment and my principles to vote for Eisenhower and Nixon, for all of the

Morningside Manifesto" was healing medicine for bruised conservatives, and their all but complete capitulation was made enthusiastic when Adlai Stevenson called the Morningside agreement "a great surrender." In the campaign, Eisenhower talked and acted like a real "States' rights" conservative.[8] When he declared at Buffalo, New York, that he would, if elected, "clean out the State Department from top to bottom," Paul Hoffman and Henry Cabot Lodge may have felt some qualms but the Conservative Americans rejoiced. Many of them said so publicly. If Ike was as good as his word, the long and tortuous lane of Roosevelt liberalism was due for a turn to the right.[9]

---

senatorial candidates and all of the Republican House candidates and to do everything possible to bring many others to the polls to do the same. I shall be glad to speak on a national broadcast at any point throughout the country to the extent of my ability.

" 'I believe General Eisenhower will be elected. A campaign based on the American principles in which he and I believe can arouse the enthusiasm of the people and if that enthusiasm is properly organized, we will bring to the polls eight million more voters than have ever voted the Republican ticket before. That is a sure program for success.' "

[8] "The Federal Government did not create the States of the Republic. The States created the Federal Government. The creation should not supersede the creator. For, if the States lose their meaning, our entire system of government loses its meaning and the next step is the rise of the centralized national state in which the seeds of autocracy can take root and grow." (Des Moines, Ia., Sept. 29, 1952.)

[9] In a speech delivered over the National Broadcasting Company network, the author of this book said:

"The old copybook maxim says that now is the time for all good men to come to the aid of their party. In the long past I have done so consistently. I earnestly wish that I might do so now. It is with the greatest reluctance that I am here to explain why I must vote against certain candidates of my party in the election next Tuesday. I am a life-long Democrat, with a passionate devotion to the political principles of Thomas Jefferson. In my judgment all of these principles radiate from Jefferson's greatest writing, if, indeed, it is not the greatest secular writing of all time, the Declaration of Independence.

"As a Democrat, I was appointed to a position of great responsibility by

President Franklin D. Roosevelt during his first administration. All of my close political associations and many of my dearest friends are active Democrats. I regret the pain that this recantation is going to cause them. Let me assure them, and let me assure you all, that it pains me too, and most acutely. I sense deeply now the meaning of the statement that the truth sometimes hurts.

"It would be personally expedient for me to keep my own counsel, and register these sentiments in the privacy of the voting booth. Millions of Democrats will do just that. But my convictions, ladies and gentlemen, are too critical, too deeply rooted and far too strong to be suppressed any longer. I had hoped that Republicans would express these convictions for me, but up to this late hour they have not done so. My conscience drives me to this personal explanation of the reason why I must now disregard parties as well as personalities, and cast my vote for the Constitution of the United States.

"Most seriously, let me assure you that behind the thick screen of campaign oratory seen and heard during the past weeks, the real issue in this election is all but totally obscured. That issue is this: Shall we scrap the Constitution of the United States, or shall we keep it? The important question is just as simple as that. As a professional witness, and for the record, I wish first to state my conviction that the election of the Democratic candidate for President would for every practical and legal purpose permanently destroy all constitutional limitations upon the power of the President, and leave the President free to do to us and with us just as he pleases. This, my friends, is tyranny. It is this awful and menacing prospect of a completely unheralded despotism that will compel me to vote for General Eisenhower. I urgently hope that you will do likewise.

"Let me presume to tell you something about the Constitution. I presume to do so for the same reason that a skilled mechanic or a machinist would presume to tell me about the nature and operation of a lathe, or a drill press. For my life's work has been the study and the teaching of the Constitution of the United States. For more than twenty-five years I was professor and teacher of Constitutional Law in one of the great universities of the country. Many of my former students are now seasoned practitioners in every state of the Union. I love and revere the Constitution for the great and singular human achievement that it climaxes.

"In our Declaration of Independence the Founding Fathers, with daring accuracy, planned and blueprinted the capture and subjugation of that elusive and often tyrannical thing called Government. Later, in the Constitution of the United States, the Founding Fathers effectively seized that government, and securely tied it down, root, stem and branch. With the past history of the world spread out before them, these founders knew, as one of them said, that government is like fire; a dangerous servant and a fearful master.

"Before their revolutionary time, the uncontrolled and apparently uncontrollable fire of government had swept back and forth over the human race, burning man's God-given freedom to a dry and painful crisp. 'It shall not happen here,' the Founding Fathers said—and so the fire of government which they lighted in the Declaration of Independence was immediately restricted and confined behind the iron walls of narrow Constitutional limitations.

"This iron structure of constitutional containment was completed in the Constitution of the United States. At that precise moment historical time stood still and literally took off its hat to a famous first in human history. Then and there, human liberty was not merely proclaimed; it was practically defined and positively guaranteed to those who were then and would subsequently be fortunate enough to be Americans. 'Liberty,' said the Founders, 'lives only in a climate of strictly limited government. Where the government is unlimited, no citizen is free.'

"It was forty years ago, during another great Presidential campaign, that the then Democratic candidate for President said this: 'The history of liberty is the history of the limitation of governmental power. When we resist the concentration of governmental power we are resisting the processes of death, because a concentration of governmental power is what always precedes the death of human freedom.' My friends, that candidate was Woodrow Wilson. If, in recent weeks, Governor Stevenson had been repeating Wilson's warning, I would not be speaking to you tonight.

"In this campaign we are promised, both by the Democratic record and by the Democratic candidate, not the limitation of governmental power, but the indefinite expansion and continued concentration of that power. In this, as Wilson warned, is the death of human freedom, and this, if you please, at a time when we are spending practically all of our effort and much more than all of our money, to defeat a similar despotic concentration of power sometimes called Communism! We are told that we can defeat this despotism in Moscow only by establishing despotism in Washington. Consciously or unconsciously, we are thus attempting to defeat Communism abroad by surrendering to it at home.

"Mark you well, my friends, the last act in this tragic dramatization of the death of American liberty and American independence will come with the complete concentration of power in the hands of the President of the United States. The stage will then be set for the great epilogue when the iron curtain falls upon the United States as it has fallen upon the so-called democracies of Eastern Europe.

"Let us please remember that the pattern of Communist conquest stands boldly revealed. It is no top secret that since the end of World War II the Russian Communist despotism has captured more than six hundred million non-Russian European and Asiatic peoples. With these people fifteen separate and formerly independent nations have disappeared behind the iron curtain. This, the greatest conquest of all history, was completed without the official loss of a single Russian soldier or the dropping of a single Russian bomb. Russia took Czechoslovakia with Czechs, Roumania with Roumanians, Bulgaria with Bulgarians, China with Chinese. Russia intends to take America with Americans!

"But first, my friends, Russia must destroy our one impregnable defense against Communism—our Constitutional system of strictly limited government divided amongst 48 separate and independent states. The revealed pattern of Russian conspiratorial conquest is simple: First they capture control— the central control—of the police of the nation to be subjugated. Next, through the activity of the police, they capture the ballot boxes; this is the way they did it in Czechoslovakia, which was one of the most progressive and most industrialized nations of Europe, whose people had an extremely high standard of living.

"But thanks to the good old Constitution, both the police and the ballot boxes here in America are controlled in 48 separate and independent places, under state laws protected by constitutionally established States' rights. Until the Communist conspirators can centralize these and other vital governmental controls that are wisely and purposely distributed amongst the states by our Constitution, they cannot possibly succeed. But they have found a way, my friends, and it is working! This brings me to the point of my confession, and of this expression of my conscientious convictions here this evening.

"It is an unfortunate fact, and one that is not too well known, that a treaty negotiated between the United States and foreign nations, becomes the supreme law of the land. A treaty so negotiated and ratified is superior to the Constitution of the United States, its Bill of Rights, the Constitution of every State of the Union, and all state and federal laws. Treaties are originated in and motivated through the State Department of our government. They are then handed to the Senate for ratification. The treaty-making process has been continuous during the last few years—ominously continuous.

"Mind you, I said that these treaties are promoted, motivated and guided by the State Department. This brings me to a matter of official record. July 24, 1950, and the event is recorded on page 10,805 of the Congressional Record for that day, Senator Ferguson of Michigan rose in the Senate and with the permission of Senator McKellar, the chairman of the Senate Committee on Appropriations, made public a memorandum which had been sent in confidence and in secret by a sub-committee of the Senate Appropriations Committee to General Marshall, then Secretary of State, three years previously; namely, on June 10, 1947. This theretofore confidential memorandum, then and there revealed by Senator Ferguson, reads in part as follows: It is from the Senate Appropriations Committee to the Secretary of State, George C. Marshall, dated June 10, 1947. I quote it:

'It becomes necessary, due to the gravity of the situation, to call your attention to a condition that developed and still flourishes in the State Department under the administration of Dean Acheson. It is evident that there is a deliberate, calculated program being carried out, not only to protect Communist personnel in high places, *but to reduce security and intelligence to a nullity.'*

"Now there are eight more paragraphs in this letter, my dear friends, replete with specifications, names and indications of persons and organizations being financed by the State Department who and which were engaged in undermining the intelligence and security of the country.

"I call your attention to the fact that this was back in 1947, when the evil administration of Dean Acheson was taken cognizance of by this important sub-committee of the Appropriations Committee of the United States Senate. Was Dean Acheson fired? On the contrary, he was promoted! And today, under this Democratic administration, Dean Acheson is one of the most important people in the world.

"This brings me to the point of my resolution. A few weeks ago, in South Bend, Indiana, one of his auditors asked Governor Stevenson a simple question. He said, 'Governor, will you fire Dean Acheson if you are elected?' Governor Stevenson replied candidly. He said, 'I will answer that question after Election Day.' A day or two later, General Eisenhower in New York picked up and quoted the question and answer that I have just told you, and then and there General Eisenhower promised, not after election day, but immediately, that he would clear out the State Department from top to bottom. I assumed that included Dean Acheson and company, and I then and there decided that I must vote for Dwight D. Eisenhower, because, my friends, the disintegration of our constitutional system, which is our first and best line of defense against conspiratorial Communism, is now being accomplished by Acheson's State Department through the promotion, negotiation, and ratification of treaties with the United States and other countries.

"This is no mere guess of mine. States are losing their powers by virtue of negotiated treaty provisions. Only a few months ago a court in California held that certain treaties recently negotiated with the United States and other countries and ratified by the Senate have suspended certain marriage laws of California. A little later a court in Idaho decided that these same recently ratified treaties had suspended the alien land laws of the State of Idaho. These are ominous forebodings of the disintegration of state constitutional jurisdiction through the treaty route. These things are all involved in the remarks of General Eisenhower and Governor Stevenson with reference to Dean Acheson.

"But the most ominous forecast of all came in the course of the steel decision. Everybody was acutely conscious of constitutional limitations when the President of the United States recently seized the steel mills. His power was challenged; the case went dramatically to the Supreme Court of the United

States and, after deliberation, the Supreme Court rendered one of the most important decisions in its entire history. The Court decided officially that the President had exceeded his constitutional powers; that his seizure of the steel mills was without warrant, and consequently the mills were returned to their owners. A great sigh of relief went over the country, and toasts were drunk to the good old Constitution.

"But there was a dissenting opinion in that case, my friends, which many people overlooked. It was written by the Chief Justice of the United States. If two more Justices had joined the Chief Justice, this decision would have been the majority opinion and it would have been the law of the land. Here is what the Chief Justice said in substance:

"He said that certain recently negotiated and recently ratified treaties between the United States and foreign countries had justified the President's seizure of the steel mills, the Constitution of the United States to the contrary notwithstanding! Ladies and gentlemen, I hope the full import of that decision hits you as it hit me. The President, by virtue of these recently negotiated treaties, has unlimited power, according to the Chief Justice, *constitutional limitations to the contrary notwithstanding*. This with reference to the treaties already ratified. There is a score of treaties awaiting ratification upon the reconvention of Congress, and if these treaties negotiated through the State Department become ratified by the Senate, not one shred of your constitutional rights or of the rights of the states will remain.

"Those of us who are acutely conscious of the establishment of Socialism in one form or another by Congressional action; others who are concerned about the rights of the states to tide-lands and to all state lands and waters, for that matter; all who are worried about the encroachment of federal legislation upon the states' control of the ballot and the states' control of police, should examine the treaties that have been negotiated and are pending ratification by the Senate—treaties that will be superior to and will supersede the Constitution of the United States. Let me tell you, ladies and gentlemen, that in that list of treaties there are provisions which affect your right to practice religion, things which affect the freedom of the press, which affect your right to hold property, things which affect the rights of labor to organize and of management to meet with employees and to discuss with them the problems of their industry—all these things to be established by treaty law in spite of the determination of Congress, and in spite of the determination of the states. Here is the Achilles heel in the body of our constitutional protections, the body that must defend us against the international Communist conspiracy which threatens us.

"A wise and thoroughly repentent ex-Communist told me in South Bend about six or eight years ago that as long as we preserve our States' rights, constitutional system intact, vigilantly and thoroughly, we need never worry about this Communist conspiracy because if our federal States' rights, constitutional system is preserved the Communist conspirators cannot do to us what they have done to other countries. He emphasized that governmental powers must first be centralized before the Communists can take them over.

"And so in this election, my dear friends, you are not voting for mere men; you are voting upon the most critical issue ever presented to the American people. Dean Acheson and Governor Stevenson are cut from the same cloth. When Governor Stevenson refused to go on record with a clear commitment on the firing of Dean Acheson I saw an endless program of Constitution-destroying treaties unfolding through the agency of this man who was criticized by the Senate Appropriations Committee way back in 1947, but who is still in supreme control of our unfortunate diplomacy.

"And so I call upon you to be vigilant. This will take not only a Republican President; it will take strong, constitutionally-minded governors, many of whom are contending seriously for election in the various states of the Union. Remember it takes a courageous governor to defend his State and the rights of his State against these federal encroachments. It also takes an *American* Senate and a thoroughly *American* House of Representatives. I urge you to look closely at the records of the men who are contending for the Senate. Elect such men as Bricker of Ohio, Malone of Nevada, Jenner of Indiana, Jim Kem here in Missouri, Goldwater of Arizona, Potter of Michigan—all of these men are vigilant, active defenders of the constitutional system and keenly conscious of the great danger that confronts us through this conspiratorial movement called Communism.

"Now, let me say a final word to my Democratic friends. I know of the difficulties with which you are presently confronted because I have lived with them myself during the past few weeks. I know that many of you secretly share my sentiments even though you will perhaps criticize my public expression of them. But I urge you to be patriots before you are Democrats. Let me say to you finally, keep your counsel, keep your silence if you must—but keep your country too. Don't let them take it away, the Constitution, I mean.

"Vote for General Dwight D. Eisenhower next Tuesday."

8

Action Defiles the Word

☆☆☆☆☆

After his first inauguration, Eisenhower continued to talk like a sincere and dedicated conservator of the Constitution. At the Conference of Governors in Seattle during the summer of 1953, the new President declared:

"I am here because of my indestructible conviction that unless we preserve in this country the place of state government with the power of authority, the responsibilities and the revenues necessary to discharge these responsibilities, then we are not going to have America as we have known it. We will have some other form of government."

This was consistent with the long string of unequivocal statements on the importance of constitutional States' rights that Eisenhower had made, going back to 1949 when he was President of Columbia University. At that time he had said:

"If we allow the constant drift toward central government to continue, ownership of property will gradually drift into the central government and finally we shall have to have dictatorship as the only means of operating such a huge organization." [1]

[1] It was Eisenhower's reputation as a convinced "States' righter" that enabled southern politicians to cut into Taft's claim upon the southern delegations

What the Earl of Rochester wrote about King Charles II of England may some day be paraphrased of Eisenhower.[2] While his syntax was frequently confused, the President's meaning was generally clear and was in the same "good father" focus of his popular image. The American people knew and most of them were glad that Ike was no fast-talking "smart alec" like his erstwhile opponent, Adlai Stevenson. The new President went to church; he was for "peace" and he preached the homely virtues, political and moral. Old fashioned States' righters were especially heartened when Eisenhower recommended and Congress promptly created a Commission on Intergovernmental Relations to explore ways and means for the emancipation of state and local governments from entrenched federal control.[3]

---

immediately before and during the 1952 Republican Convention. The same reputation was largely responsible for the big popular vote that Ike received all over the South in the November election of that year which enabled him to carry Virginia, Texas, Tennessee and Florida.

2 "Here lies our sovereign lord the King, whose word no man relies on; he never says a foolish thing nor ever does a wise one." These lines are said to have been written on the door of the King's bedchamber.

3 On August 18, 1953, President Eisenhower announced the appointment of this author as chairman of the new Commission on Intergovernmental Relations. The appointment was received with enthusiasm by the nation's press:

Indianapolis Star editorial, August 20, 1953: "The choice of Clarence Manion as chairman of the new Commission on Federal-State relationship is an eloquent tribute to the deeply felt sentiment among Hoosiers for a return to the maximum self-rule for the states and local communities in the face of steadily encroaching federal power. . . . At every step of the way some entrenched bureaucrat is bound to squawk. But to Manion and Hoover we say, 'More power to you.' "

Yakima Republic, Yakima, Washington, August 20, 1953: "It was only two weeks ago that President Eisenhower told the governors of forty-eight states in their Seattle Conference that he would immediately tackle the problem of overlapping federal-state relations. It is pleasing to see the President follow through with his appointment of a chairman for his Commission. . . . Clarence Manion, his appointee, will be regarded widely as an excellent choice for the chairmanship of such an important committee. He has spoken across the nation in past days of the 'Fair Deal' urging an end to waste in govern-

But Mr. Eisenhower's actions soon belied his words. Persons who were in a position to observe him closely in those days were convinced that the President was naïvely unaware

ment. Many at the time may have thought him a voice in the wilderness, but now the nation is seeing different times. . . . The President's appointee is already toeing the mark, ready to perform a great service for the United States."

Memphis Commercial Appeal, August 25, 1953: "Mark down the name of Clarence Manion who has been named head of a Commission to study relations between state government and federal government. . . . The name of Manion will, without doubt, be abused from many quarters. It can emerge as a big name in the continuing struggle to maintain the strength of government by the people."

Houston Post editorial, August 24, 1953: "President Eisenhower has chosen a pre-eminently well-qualified man for an important job in appointing Clarence Manion chairman of the newly created Commission to study federal-state relations. Mr. Manion is a top-flight lawyer and an authority on government and constitutional law. . . . Spearheaded by a chairman of Mr. Manion's caliber and views, the Commission on Intergovernmental Relations may be expected to present a blueprint that may well lead to government reforms of the first magnitude."

Houston Chronicle, editorial, August 24, 1953: "President Eisenhower made a good choice in naming Clarence Manion chairman of the new Commission to study federal-state relationships. Dean Manion is a competent student of government, especially its legal phases. He is not identified with any particular political faction and can give non-partisan leadership to the move to restore the balance between the federal government and the states, ignored by federal officials promoting an all-powerful centralized government. That trend must be reversed."

Los Angeles Times, August 20, 1953: "The appointment of Clarence Manion, a distinguished lawyer and former Dean of the Notre Dame Law School, to head the Commission on federal-state problems is a good one. Mr. Manion, who has spoken on behalf of the Bricker Amendment for the American Bar Association, is a student of government and should be thoroughly qualified."

Indianapolis News, August 20, 1953: "In appointing Clarence Manion as chairman of the Commission on Intergovernmental Relations, President Eisenhower has drawn on eminent qualifications and sound viewpoint. His (Manion's) chairmanship of a committee to study and recommend on intergovernmental powers gives authority and prestige to the whole undertaking."

Buffalo, N.Y. Evening News, August 21, 1953: "President Eisenhower has chosen well in putting Clarence Manion, former Dean of the Notre Dame Law School, as head of his new Commission on Intergovernmental Relations.

of the great variance that existed between the policies of
his administration and the pronouncements that he was still
making about the evils of big centralized government.[4] One

Manion has gained wide recognition in the last few years as one of the most
brilliant advocates of what might be called a modern philosophy of Constitutional Conservatism. An ardent supporter of Senator Taft before the 1952
Republican Convention, he was regarded as certain to be included in a Taft
Cabinet. His grasp of the legal and constitutional complexities of intergovernmental relationship should fit him well for this new assignment."

Washington Post, August 23, 1953: "Clarence Manion's support of the
Bricker Amendment to curb the President's treaty-making power is certainly
not a favorable omen for the study he is to direct into intergovernmental
relations. Senator Bricker's proposal would shift to the states, power that can
be properly exercised only by the President, acting with the consent of the
Senate. It is the worst threat to a reasonable division of local and the national powers that has risen in recent years. If the commission were to follow
Mr. Manion in this effort to turn back the clock in our international relations, everything else it might attempt probably would be lost in the resulting
confusion."

Chicago Tribune editorial, October 2, 1953: "An address in Boston by Dr.
Clarence Manion, former Dean of the Notre Dame Law School, convinces us
that Dr. Manion is going to do a job as chairman of the Commission on
Intergovernmental affairs appointed by Mr. Eisenhower. . . .

"Dr. Manion said that Constitutional safeguards have been liquidated
steadily during the last thirty years because of the 'complacent irresponsibility of the American people.' They have allowed a headstrong executive
branch, a power-grabbing bureaucracy and politically activated courts to make
great progress in building up centralized governmental authority.

"To Dr. Manion, the concentration of power in the federal branch is all
wrong. The greatest obstacle to Communist conspirators, he said, is the de-
centralization of power and decentralized jurisdictions established by the
Constitution. It is hard to seize police powers and ballot boxes in forty-eight
different jurisdictions. . . .

"Dr. Manion has demonstrated an appreciation of the fundamental task in
preserving individual liberty against big government. The more he can do
to bring the central government down to size, and to whittle away its sphere
of jurisdiction and its impersonal power, the better off we all shall be."

[4] At the White House on December 15, 1953, I told the President that the
proposed expansion of federal programs announced by Nelson A. Rockefeller,
Undersecretary of Health, Education and Welfare, and others would embar-
rass the work of the Intergovernmental Relations Commission and conflict
with Mr. Eisenhower's forthright pronouncements on the subject of States'

of his first recommendations to Congress called for the creation of an additional Cabinet office charged with the supervision of the nation's health, education and welfare. It was ironical that the Commission on Intergovernmental Relations was lodged in the sprawling edifice that housed this huge new federal encroachment upon the reserved rights of the states. The subjects of health, education and welfare are all kept in the exclusive dominion of the several state governments under the terms of the Tenth Amendment to the Constitution. Aside from their impacts upon interstate commerce, the only federal approach to these areas is through Congressional appropriations made to provide for "the general welfare of the United States." Since the Supreme Court had already declared that a taxpayer is powerless to challenge the relationship of a particular Congressional appropriation to the general welfare of the country,[5] and that the federal government may regulate anything that it subsidizes,[6] the new Cabinet office opened a wide door for the invasion and the preemption of state jurisdiction by the bribes of a burgeoning bureaucracy.[7]

Another casualty in the battle for States' rights inside the Eisenhower administration was in the field of highway con-

---

rights. I informed him that this was the opinion of people who had supported him in 1952 on the basis of these States' rights promises.

The President was indignant. He demanded the names of such people. When I supplied them, he relegated them all to "the political vintage of 1873" and ended the interview with a desk-pounding denunciation of reactionaries who refused to recognize the realities of the present time and the virtues of the middle of the road.

5 *Frothingham v. Mellon,* 262 U.S. 447, 1923.

6 *Wickard v. Filburn,* 317 U.S. 111, 1942.

7 The new Department of Health, Education and Welfare combined the existing activities of the Pure Food and Drug Administration, the Surgeon General's Office, the Federal Department of Education, and the Social Security Administration, with a total employment of 35,000 people in 1953. In 1962, the number of employees exceeded 73,000.

struction. This was the first consideration to which the Commission on Intergovernmental Relations addressed itself. In 1953 the Commission assigned the subject to a study committee of ten distinguished highway specialists from all parts of the country. At the same time the transportation division of the Department of Commerce was making its own investigation in close co-ordination with the studies being made by the Intergovernmental Relations Commission. In all important respects the concluding recommendations of the Department of Commerce and the study committee of the Commission were the same, namely:

A. Federal aid to state highway construction and maintenance should be discontinued and the responsibility for such highway construction and maintenance should be left to the states.
B. Federal excise taxes on gasoline and other motor fuel should be removed.
C. The federal government should assume sole responsibility for the construction and maintenance of highways on federally owned areas and reservations and in places where its activities and military installations place greatly increased burdens on state roads.
D. The Federal Bureau of Roads should be stripped of its administrative functions but should be continued as a research organization and as a reservoir for technical information and advice.

These recommendations were formally presented by its study committee to the full Commission on Intergovernmental Relations on February 17, 1954, and accepted by the Commission with an enthusiastic vote of thanks and appreciation for the study committee's work. In the meantime, however, the identical recommendations by the Department of Commerce had been vetoed by Presidential Assistant Sherman Adams for the expressed reason that the Eisenhower administration was in "political trouble" and needed big spending programs to get it out. The Secretary of Commerce was consequently directed to prepare a federal highway spending proposal that would be larger and more expensive than that presented to Congress by any previous administration. The Adams directive was duly accomplished and the results are in the record.[8]

By the time it rendered its final report (June 20, 1955), the Commission on Intergovernmental Relations had conveniently gutted the findings of its study committee and recommended instead that "the present federal aid highway program be continued and that funds appropriated thereunder be increased." [9]

[8] "The American people in 1956 were sold a beautiful 27-billion dollar dream—a 40,000-mile super-highway network that would sweep majestically from coast to coast and border to border. This greatest engineering project of all time would, we were told, be a splendid monument to a free people's wisdom, daring, foresight and skill. . . . What was more, it would pay for itself painlessly out of our federal taxes on tires and our three-cents-a-gallon federal gasoline tax. Today, the dream has become a nightmare of recklessness, extravagance, special privilege, bureaucratic stupidity and sometimes outright thievery. The entire network was originally scheduled to cost 27 billion dollars (but) within two years the official figure was quietly raised to 40 billion. . . . Meanwhile the federal gas tax has climbed to four cents and Congress is considering another hike. The federal government simply shovels out the money for the states to spend." *Readers Digest,* July, 1960.

[9] To this portion of the report the following footnote is appended:

"Mr. Burton, Governors Thornton, Jones and Shivers, Senator Schoeppel and Congressman Doliver join in the following statement:

" 'We regretfully dissent from this major highway recommendation by the Commission. The recommendation endorses a permanent direction we believe to be unsound. . . .'

"Governors Driscoll and Battle dissent as follows:

" 'We must dissent from the Commission's recommendation for an increase in highway grants. . . . Responsibility for the construction and maintenance of a modern nation-wide highway system should rest with the states. . . . The federal government has sought to control wages, establish national standards, choose routes, and to control the use of margin areas along federally aided highways. Any increase in highway grants can be expected to increase

There was strong dissent among Commission members but the arm of Mr. Sherman Adams was very strong and far reaching in those days, and on the second time around, he had made no mistake in the selection of a chairman for the Commission on Intergovernmental Relations.[10]

The 1952 Republican platform recognized that federal spending is the measure of the size and strength of the central government. It condemned "the wanton extravagance and inflationary spending policies of the Truman administration, which along with the most confiscatory taxes in history made effective control of government expenditures impossible." Consequently, the platform promised a reduction of federal spending, the elimination of waste and a balanced budget as a prerequisite for general tax reduction.[11]

---

the budgetary impact and further curtail the fiscal independence of the states. *. . . The present federal gasoline tax should be repealed. . . .* The funds required to support the grant-in-aid device are collected from the citizens of the states. The states with the greatest density of population, the greatest highway needs, and the largest number of highway accidents are likewise the states whose citizens make the largest contribution to the federal treasury. These are also the states to which the largest highway grants will be given. *This unnecessary and wasteful exchange of tax dollars inevitably strengthens the centralization of our government in Washington. In fact the grant-in-aid programs that have been proposed are more likely to strengthen the centralized bureaucracy than to speed highway construction. . . . By the same token they weaken the state and local governments.'* "

House Document 198, 84th Congress, 1st session, U.S. Government Printing Office.

10 "President Eisenhower today named Meyer Kestnbaum of Chicago, a clothing firm executive, as the new chairman of the Government Commission on federal-state problems.

"Kestnbaum, President of Hart, Schaffner and Marx, and also the chairman of the Committee for Economic Development, succeeds Clarence Manion who left the Commission last February 24, saying that the White House had asked for his resignation. Kestnbaum, 57, will take the oath of office as the Committee's new chairman at the White House ceremonies tomorrow afternoon and Eisenhower will be present." *Associated Press*, April 21, Augusta, Georgia.

11 Republican Platform for 1952: *"Taxation and Monetary Policy. . . .* We advocate the following tax policies: (1) Reduction of expenditures by the

In the Morningside Manifesto[12] Taft had said and Eisenhower had agreed that "the greatest threat to liberty today is internal from the constant growth of the government through the constantly increasing power and expansion of the federal government." Both Taft and Eisenhower had then agreed that the "price of continued liberty including a free economic system is the reduction of federal spending and taxes, the repudiation of arbitrary powers in the executive and a stand against statutory extension of power by the creation and extension of federal bureaus."

Three months after Ike's inauguration,[13] at a White House conference of legislative leaders and Cabinet officers, Taft learned that these anti-spending pledges were to be forgotten. At this meeting the President disclosed his budgetary recommendations which indicated that heavy deficit spending would continue and that the first Republican budget would be out of balance. Taft's response was explosive. He pointed out that the net result of the Eisenhower administration to date was the continuation of spending on the same old Truman scale. The projected budget total, which exceeded 30 per cent of the national income, was condemned by Taft as outrageous.

"The one primary thing we promised the American people," he shouted, "was reduction of expenditures. Now you're taking us down the same road Truman traveled. It's a repudiation of everything we promised in the campaign." He added that he was certain that Republican candidates

---

elimination of waste and extravagance so that the budget will be balanced and a general tax reduction can be made. (2) An immediate study directed toward reallocation of fields of taxation between the federal, state and municipal governments so as to allow greater fiscal freedom to the states and municipalities, thus minimizing double taxation and enabling the various divisions of government to meet their obligations more efficiently."

12 See p. 84 supra.

13 April 30, 1953.

would go down to defeat in 1954 unless the program was changed. An official reporter of this critical incident says, "In retrospect it is not difficult to imagine what a grevious political storm would have broken over the President's head if Taft had walked out on that meeting and denounced the budget on the outside as he had on the inside, and launched a movement against Eisenhower's military and foreign policies." [14]

This was not the first discrepancy that Taft had encountered in Ike's promises as a candidate on the one hand and his performance as President on the other. During the campaign, Eisenhower had declared that if elected, he "would clean out the State Department from top to bottom." The President's method of suiting action to these cheering words was to nominate Charles E. Bohlen as United States ambassador to the Soviet Union. Bohlen was a career man in the State Department and in the popular mind was typical of those whom Eisenhower had promised to "clean out." Furthermore, the Republican platform had called Roosevelt's Yalta Agreement, "An aid to Communist enslavement," and had promised to repudiate it and "all other such secret understandings." Along with Alger Hiss, Bohlen had attended the Yalta Conference, where he acted as Roosevelt's translator. At critical moments in the Yalta discussions, he, Roosevelt and Hiss were the only Americans present with Stalin and the Russians. While his nomination by Eisenhower was under consideration, Bohlen stoutly defended the Yalta Agreement before the Senate Foreign Relations Committee and this raised a storm of disapproval in the Congress.

While Taft was unhappy over the President's incredible selection of Bohlen, he nevertheless realized that Senate rejection of the appointment would give the new Republican

[14] *Eisenhower: The Inside Story*, by Robert J. Donovan (Harper & Bros., New York, 1956), p. 109.

adminstration's prestige a severe blow. He consequently salvaged it with a bipartisan arrangement whereby he and Senator Sparkman of Alabama read Bohlen's F.B.I. file and agreed for publication that it contained no reflection upon Bohlen's loyalty to the United States. The Senate then confirmed Bohlen's appointment by a vote of 74 to 13. But Taft had had enough. He sent word to the White House: "No more Bohlens." [15]

How long would Taft remain loyally harnessed to Eisenhower's continued violations of the Republican party's pledged word? The Senator's tragic death from cancer on July 31, stayed the answer to that question.

Taft's death was the first and most important in a long series of casualties suffered by the big conservative majority that ruled the Senate when Eisenhower was first inaugurated. Death, as in the case of Taft, McCarren, McCarthy, and Butler of Nebraska, figured in these losses, but demoralization and/or defeat took an even greater toll. Stalwarts like Knowland, Bridges, Bricker, Goldwater, Ferguson, Jenner, Malone, Schoeppel, Welker, Butler of Maryland, and others, were effectively disarmed, immobilized and censored, if not silenced completely, by the "progressive moderation" of their party's leader in the White House. These Senators would have pilloried and paralyzed a Stevenson or a Truman for proposing what they were required to swallow and support when it was presented and plugged by their own party's President.

The end result was the all but complete collapse of the American nationalism and constitutional conservation that had characterized the Republican party throughout its history. These frustrated forces of Americanism that had won the election for Eisenhower in 1952 had become a shambles

15 *The Taft Story,* by William Smith White (Harper & Brothers, New York, 1954), p. 239.

by 1960. All the figures revealed it. Truman had budgeted 40 billion dollars for all expenses of the federal government in 1950. Ike budgeted twice that amount, 80 billion, that is, for 1960. He had thus become the all-time high-spending peace-time Presidential champion of the world.[16]

Richard Nixon, the Republican Presidential candidate in 1960, who had made his Congressional reputation as a militant anti-Communist conservative, was fatally blighted by his official association and identification with the Eisenhower record of big spending, internationalism and Communist appeasement.

The men who "drafted" Ike in 1952 had picked him for a role that no other person could have played. No President but Eisenhower could have doubled the expenditures of his prodigal predecessor and continued to talk about the virtues of economy and pose as one who practiced it. Without the personal prestige of Eisenhower's unflagging support, foreign aid would have ended long ago and in the absence of Eisenhower's fixation about "peace," successful anti-Communist revolution behind the Iron Curtain, which the Republican Platform of 1952 promised to encourage, would have swept all Communist governments from the face of the earth before 1956.

If anybody but Eisenhower had been President of the United States in 1954, the Bricker Amendment with its essential "which clause" would be a part of the Constitution

16 "The fiscal situation deteriorated faster in the past 18 months than in any comparable time period to my knowledge. . . . At the present rate federal agencies would spend approximately 400 billion dollars within the next five years. *Contrary to general understanding, recent great increases in federal spending have not been for defense or 'foreign aid.' The tremendous increases have been for home-civilian programs.* Since 1954, expenditures outside of defense, atomic energy and foreign aid categories increased from 19 billion to 34 billion estimated in the current year. . . . This is an increase of 14.9 billion or 78 per cent in five years. . . ."
Manion Forum Broadcast, Senator Harry Byrd, June 21, 1959.

today and its distinguished and scholarly author would still be a member of the United States Senate. Ike defeated the Bricker Amendment narrowly (one Senate vote) but effectively all by himself.

No President but Eisenhower could have rescued General Zwicker from the investigation by Senator McCarthy and thus stopped forever an answer to the question, "Who Promoted Major Peress?" [17]

If Truman or any other President but Eisenhower had invited the "Butcher of Budapest" to Camp David and to the White House, impeachment proceedings would have been started against him in the House of Representatives.

All of this was a large order for a mortal man, but Ike accomplished it with the continuous support of nation-wide press agentry which played down what the President was actually doing, and projected his benevolent image as the "Man of Peace," the image which the American people learned to love. If the Constitution had permitted it, the Republicans, so-called, would have nominated Eisenhower for a third term in 1960 and he would have been elected "hands down."

When Eisenhower prepared to leave office, the conservative Republican leadership that had flourished so militantly with such bright promise in 1952 had all but disappeared. With the exception of Senator Barry Goldwater, there was little or no uncompromising conservatism left at the top of the party, but there was a big ground swell of it at the bottom as Mr. Nixon discovered at the 1960 Republican Convention. It was too late at that time for Nixon to do anything about it. His "I agree with Senator Kennedy, but . . ." left the conservatives cold, and millions of them refused to vote for anybody for President.[18]

[17] *U.S. News and World Report,* Nov. 12, 1954, p. 132.
[18] "IGNORED BOTH NIXON AND KENNEDY: More than 50,000 Chi-

As conservatives picked up the pieces after the wreckage of the 1960 election, some of them recalled the old saw from John Gay's Fables:

> "An open foe may prove a curse
> But a pretended friend is worse." [19]

Amen!

---

cagoans who voted in Tuesday's election failed or refused to mark their ballots for either Presidential candidate, an analysis of the voting records disclosed Thursday. This was enough to have swung the state solidly either way in a race in which Senator Kennedy's once commanding lead over Vice-President Nixon now stands at 5,524. In Chicago, 1,719,592 ballots were cast. Kennedy drew 1,060,173 and Nixon 604,820 for a total of 1,664,993 votes.

"This means that 54,599 persons didn't vote for either."

Article by William F. Mooney in Red Streak Edition of *Chicago Daily News,* Thursday, Nov. 10, 1960.

[19] Part 1, Par. 17.

9

The Menace of Treaty Law

☆☆☆☆☆

The 1952 Republican platform contained the following pledge:

"We shall see to it that no treaty or agreement with other countries deprives our citizens of the rights guaranteed them by the Federal Constitution."

A studied second reading of this promise will leave many American citizens puzzled and incredulous. The statement is a frank acknowledgment of the fact that the rights guaranteed by the Constitution are now subject to violation by a treaty or an agreement between our government and a foreign government. Persons unacquainted with the subject always find this statement hard to believe.

In the popular campaign for the adoption of what came to be called the Bricker Constitutional Amendment, the first job of every speaker was to convince his audience that the menace of treaty law actually existed.[1] It was all but incon-

[1] The movement for an amendment to the Constitution to protect American rights and the American form of government against the dangers of "Treaty Law" was originated in 1948 by Frank E. Holman, who was then president of the American Bar Association. As the result of an intensive speaking and writing campaign led by Mr. Holman, the House of Delegates of the Ameri-

ceivable to the average American that any authority, foreign or domestic, could deprive him of his constitutional rights with impunity. Practically everybody knew that laws passed by Congress and state legislatures must conform to the Constitution, and if these laws did not so conform then the courts would set them aside as invalid. Most Americans knew about their constitutional immunities from unreasonable searches, self-incrimination and such, and they also knew that the police and others could be forced to respect these constitutional protections. They were unfriendly to the suggestion that a treaty with a foreign nation could impair these time-honored protections and when they first heard about the proposed Bricker amendment they were strongly inclined to believe that it was unnecessary.

In February, 1952, United States Senator John W. Bricker of Ohio introduced in the Senate a resolution (S.J. 130) which was designed to establish the safeguard called for by the American Bar Association. Senator Bricker's resolution was referred to the Judiciary Committee of the Senate which conducted hearings on the proposal during the Spring of 1952. Action on the proposed amendment lapsed with the adjournment of Congress in the summer of 1952.

On January 7, 1953, Senator Bricker and sixty-three other Senators introduced another resolution (S.J. Res. # 1) for an amendment to protect constitutional rights against treaty

---

can Bar Association at its mid-winter meeting in Chicago in February, 1952, passed the following resolution:

"The American Bar Association recommends to the Congress of the United States for consideration an amendment to the Constitution of the United States in respect of the treaty-making power reading as follows:

"'A provision of a treaty which conflicts with any provision of this Constitution shall not be of any force and effect. A treaty shall become effective as internal law in the United States only through legislation by Congress which it could enact under its delegated powers in the absence of such a treaty.'"

law. Senator Arthur Watkins of Utah later introduced another such resolution (S.J. # 3) in language more closely
conforming to the resolution of the American Bar Association. In June, 1953, after extended public hearings, the Senate Judiciary Committee favorably reported the following
resolutions to the Senate floor for passage:

Section 1. A provision of a treaty which conflicts with this Constitution shall not be of any force or effect.

Section 2. A treaty shall become effective as internal law in the
United States only through legislation which would
be valid in the absence of treaty.

Section 3. Congress shall have power to regulate all executive
and other agreements with any foreign power or international organization. All such agreements shall be
subject to the limitations imposed on treaties by this
article.

From the very beginning of our constitutional law the subject of treaties with foreign nations has raised involved and
difficult questions. The pertinent and sometimes conflicting
Supreme Court decisions stretch back over more than a
hundred years. But the lurking menace of treaty law to constitutional States' rights was clarified and sharpened in the
decision of *Missouri v. Holland* in 1920, and in 1942 in the
decision of *United States v. Pink,* it was extended to include
private executive agreements between our Presidents and
the representatives of foreign governments.[2]

When we joined the United Nations in 1945, we were immediately exposed to a score of international "covenants,"
"declarations," and "pacts," many of which reached into the
local and personal affairs of American life. These multilateral agreements, while international in form, were intra-
national in their operation and effect. Their impact was not

[2] See Chapter 3, note 12, supra.

upon the government of the United States merely, but upon individual citizens of this country for whom they made new laws and regulations which, according to the cases cited above, would supersede the Constitutions, laws and ordinances of the states and of the United States. It was the pending ratification of these United Nations agreements that sparked the drive for the Bricker Amendment and, considering the involved and technical nature of the proposal, the favorable public response to the campaign for its adoption was truly phenomenal.[3]

---

[3] Hundreds of state and local organizations of all kinds, and many state legislatures passed resolutions urging Congress to propose the Bricker Amendment to the states for adoption. In the 1953 public hearings on the amendment by the Senate-Judiciary Committee which lasted for several months, lawyers, laymen, and official representatives of many organizations presented their views. The following organizations appeared and endorsed the amendment:

American Legion
American Farm Bureau Federation
American Medical Association
American Medical Association, Women's Auxiliary
American Council of Christian Churches
Association of American Physicians and Surgeons
American Flag Committee
American Progress Foundation
Catholic War Veterans
Colonial Dames of America
Chamber of Commerce of the United States
Constitutional Foundation, Inc.
Committee for Constitutional Government
Conference of State Manufacturers' Associations
Conference of American Small Business Organizations
Freedom Clubs, Inc.
General Federation of Women's Clubs
Junior Order of United American Mechanics
Kiwanis, International
Marine Corps League
Military Order of the World Wars
Minute Women of U.S.A. Inc.
National Society, Daughters of the American Revolution
National Society, Sons of the American Revolution

After Eisenhower's election in 1952, it was generally expected that the Bricker Amendment would sail through Congress without appreciable difficulty. Sixty-four senators, including Senator Bricker, joined in the introduction of a new proposal for it, (Sen. Res. # 1) as soon as Congress convened in January, 1953. The sixty-four Senate supporters constituted the required two-thirds of the Senate and with the support of these sponsors alone, the amendment's passage through the Senate was assured.

No objection from the State Department was anticipated.

National Sojourners, Inc.
National Cotton Compress and Warehouse Association
National Association of Pro-America
National Association of Evangelicals
National Society for Constitutional Security
National Economic Council, Inc.
National Labor-Management Council on Foreign Trade Policy
National Small Business Association
National Association of Real Estate Boards
National Defense League of America
National Association of Life Underwriters
National Grange
Patriotic Women of America, Inc.
Steuben Society of America
Southern States Industrial Council
United Spanish War Veterans
United States Flag Committee
Veterans of Foreign Wars of the United States
Women's National Patriotic Conference on National Defense.
    The following organizations appeared and opposed the Amendment:
Americans for Democratic Action
American Jewish Congress
American Federation of Labor (International Officers)
American Association for the United Nations
American Civil Liberties Union
American Association of University Women
Association of the Bar for the City of New York (This was the only Bar Association to oppose the Amendment)
B'nai B'rith
United World Federalists.

John Foster Dulles, the new Secretary of State, had furnished the most impressive argument for the amendment in a speech delivered in Louisville, Kentucky, on April 12, 1952, when he said:

"The treaty-making power is an extraordinary power, liable to abuse. Treaties make international law and also they make domestic law. Under our Constitution, treaties become the Supreme Law of the Land. They are indeed more supreme than ordinary laws, for Congressional laws are invalid if they do not conform to the Constitution, whereas treaty laws can over-ride the Constitution. Treaties, for example, can take powers away from the Congress and give them to the President. They can take powers from the states and give them to the federal government or to some international body and *they can cut across the rights given to the people by their Constitutional Bill of Rights.*" [4] (Italics added.)

The Constitution gives the President of the United States no part in the proposal or ratification of amendments to the Constitution. The process is left entirely in the hands of Congress and the states.[5] George Washington neither took any action nor made any recommendations with reference to the proposal and ratification of the first ten amendments which were added to the Constitution during his first administration, although each of them prescribed sharp and

[4] Although Mr. Dulles later opposed the adoption of the Bricker Amendment, he never denied the accuracy of this frightening analysis that he had made at Louisville. On the contrary, when he was asked about it during his appearance before the Senate Judiciary Committee on April 6, 1953, with Mr. Herman Pfleger of San Francisco, the new legal adviser to the State Department at his elbow, he merely assured the Committee that the Eisenhower administration had no plans to make any treaties that would do the startling things he had described at Louisville. On the basis of that assurance, he insisted that no Constitutional Amendment such as Senator Bricker proposed was necessary or desirable.

[5] Article V, United States Constitution.

specific limitations upon federal power. In like manner until 1953, each and all of Washington's successors in the Presidency had remained aloof from the controversy attending the addition of amendments to the Constitution during their respective administrations. There had been no indication that President Eisenhower intended to break this long-standing precedent. On the contrary, he gave at least one firm and early assurance that he expected to observe it in the case of the pending proposal for the Bricker Amendment.

On February 25, 1953, Mr. Frank Holman, past president of the American Bar Association and Mr. Alfred J. Schweppe, then chairman of the Peace and Law Committee of that organization, had an appointment with the President which had been arranged for them by the President's brother, Mr. Edgar Eisenhower. They conferred with the President about the resolution which Senator Bricker and sixty-three other senators had introduced a month earlier as Senate Resolution # 1. Here is Mr. Holman's published account of that interview:

"The President made two propositions quite clear to us: First, that he was not in favor of treaties or international agreements overriding the Constitution of the United States, and, second, that since under our constitutional procedure, the matter of a constitutional amendment did not come to his desk for approval, *he saw no reason for taking any position on the matter.*" [6]

Mr. Holman properly and promptly spread word of the President's position through Congress and notified the appropriate people in the Departments of Justice and State. Letters and telegrams favoring the amendment were pouring in upon Congress by the thousands. The most important patriotic and professional organizations in the country were

6 *The Story of the Bricker Amendment,* Frank E. Holman. (The Committee for Constitutional Government, 205 E. 42nd St., New York 17.) $1.00.

on record favoring ratification. Only liberals and internationalists were heard in opposition.[7] Thus among other considerations in its favor, the measure appeared to be "good politics" by a preponderant ratio. At this point early congressional approval of the Bricker Amendment appeared to be definitely "in the cards."

Then somebody "lowered the boom." The first warning came from the newly appointed legal adviser to the State Department, one Herman Pfleger of San Francisco. As soon as he reached Washington he notified Frank Holman that there would be no constitutional amendment on the subject of treaty law. It is apparent now that Mr. Pfleger had told the new Secretary of State, John Foster Dulles, the same thing. Whatever the source of Mr. Pfleger's authority or certainty, the resulting turnabout was sensational.

When Secretary Dulles opposed the amendment before the Senate Judiciary Committee on April 6, some of the senators present expressed astonishment that he should oppose the amendment in view of his Louisville statement on the subject of treaty law.[8] Although he was obviously nettled by the questioning, Mr. Dulles neither denied the truth of what he had said at Louisville nor withdrew his opposition to the proposal of Senator Bricker to forestall the evil possibilities that he himself had so graphically described. Before the Committee the next day, April 7, the Attorney General, Herbert Brownell, echoed Mr. Dulles' opposition. The administration had now taken Mr. Pfleger's position that there must be no amendment at all on the subject of treaty law. There was no longer any question about it.

But that was a notoriously unpopular position as the administration soon discovered. The Senate Judiciary Committee favored the proposal by a two to one ratio and the Senate

7 Ibid.
8 John Foster Dulles, Speech in Louisville, Ky., April 12, 1952, vide supra.

was ready to approve the Committee's recommendation as soon as it reached the floor. Facing defeat on its "no amendment" position, the White House elected to delay and confuse the issue by offering to withdraw its opposition if the language of the amendment was revised. To this end the administration arranged conferences between the Attorney General, Senator Bricker and representatives of the State Department. Senator Bricker soon discovered that the administration would not accept language in the amendment which would effectively reverse the rule established in the decision of *Missouri v. Holland* (supra). This involved the "which clause," the very heart of the amendment. This clause was designed to reinforce the Tenth Amendment against any treaties dealing with the internal domestic law of the United States. Senator Bricker quite properly refused to "compromise" this vital issue and suggested that it be debated on the floor of the Senate.

Unable to "compromise" Senator Bricker, the administration negotiators then proceeded to compromise Senator William Knowland, the Republican Senate leader, who was a co-author and strong supporter of the Bricker proposal. To get itself out of the unpopular "no Bricker Amendment" position, the White House persuaded Senator Knowland to introduce a substitute resolution, which he did, without notice to Senator Bricker, on July 22.[9]

9 "On Tuesday afternoon, July 21, 1953, after the last meeting of the (negotiating) committee, Dean Clarence Manion had a talk with the Attorney General about the Bricker Amendment, following an appointment the afternoon of that day on a wholly different matter. The Attorney General did not intimate to him even late that afternoon that the administration proposed to introduce an amendment of its own. But the sudden introduction of an amendment the next day, July 22, was probably largely animated by the fact that on the preceding afternoon, Dean Manion advised the Attorney General that the people of the country were so aroused over the administration's attitude of 'no amendment' that criticism of the administration would mount during the intervening months if its attempt to stall any

Obviously this was done to redeem the administration in the estimation of the American people and to create the impression that the administration people favored the principle of the amendment, but were dissatisfied with Senator Bricker's choice of language. The Knowland substitute was referred to the Senate Judiciary Committee for further hearings which necessarily postponed a vote on the measure until Congress convened after the summer recess in January, 1954. On its face, the Knowland substitute was completely inadequate to provide the protection that was needed to ward off the danger that Mr. Dulles had so clearly described but it served the purpose of popular confusion and accomplished the delay which was what the administration badly needed to accomplish its real objective, namely, to defeat the passage of any anti-treaty amendment, however it was phrased.

During the Congressional recess, the administration continued to put forth feelers for compromise versions of the amendment using Senator Ferguson of Michigan as its emissary. But when Senator Bricker on January 31, 1954, announced that he would accept the Ferguson version if the administration would back and support it, President Eisenhower announced the next day, February 1, that he would not accept the Ferguson proposal. Thus the impasse was back where it started when Congress began to vote on the proposals on February 25.

---

amendment was continued; that he, Manion, a Democrat, had supported President Eisenhower in his election campaign specifically and publicly on the basis of the Republican platform urging a treaty amendment; that he and others expected the administration to quit stalling on this matter. In a desire to avoid this charge of stalling, and on the following day, the Knowland substitute was introduced, wholly without the knowledge of Senator Bricker, and, moreover, when he was not even present in the Senate."

The Story of the Bricker Amendment, Frank E. Holman. (The Committee for Constitutional Government, New York), p. 46.

By a vote of 61 to 30 the Senate substituted a proposed version, prepared by Senator George of Georgia, for the text reported to the floor by the Judiciary Committee, but one hour later on a vote for final passage, the George proposal failed to secure the necessary two-thirds by one vote, the vote being 60 "for" and 31 "against." Thus by the skin of its political teeth, the White House fight for "no amendment on treaty laws" was won.

Why did the Eisenhower administration wage this strange and bitter crusade against an immensely popular measure which was designed to carry out a plain promise in the Republican platform? For the answer one must reach back to the reason why Senator Taft was defeated for the Republican nomination for President in 1952: *the Bricker Amendment would have firmly re-established the national independence of the United States.*

With the Bricker Amendment it would be impossible to surrender our sovereignty and our federal form of government through adherence by treaty to international organizations. As against the United Nations or other such supranational bodies, the Bricker Amendment would have imposed the same restrictions against the power of international organizations that the Tenth Amendment now imposes against our own federal government.

In sum, the Bricker Amendment drew a sharp line of demarcation between those who believe that personal rights protected by the Constitution should not be sacrificed to international plans and purposes, and those who believe that such a sacrifice should and must be made in the interest of international co-operation. In 1954 the great majority of the American people and the great—almost two-thirds—majority of the United States Senate were on the side of nationalism and continued constitutional rights. The liberals were on the other side. The opposition of the liberals would have made no difference, but somehow they pressured President Eisenhower onto their side and this made all the difference in the world.

Goaded on by whomsoever it was, President Eisenhower fought the Bricker Amendment bitterly right down to his hairline victory on the Senate floor. In his frantic approach to the finish line, he exhausted every political resource and turned over every suspicious stone in sight. This frenetic and unprecedented interference by a President of the United States with the constitutional amending process was then and remains now inexplicable. This mystery is underscored when it is remembered that in its substance the Bricker Amendment was nothing more than a form of insurance for the continuation of American sovereignty. It would have provided a visible shield against the direct or indirect management of our domestic affairs by foreign governments. Its defeat therefore served to highlight a determination by its opponents to keep this country vulnerable to foreign intervention. This is why the full documentation of the Eisenhower struggle against the Bricker Amendment will make an important and revealing footnote to history. A small sample of that documentation is essential in this narrative on the care, feeding and frustration of American convervatism.[10]

10 From an article by Marquis Childs in the *Denver Post,* Wednesday, Nov. 7, 1953: "In view of the seriousness with which the administration regards this issue, (the Bricker Amendment) it is all the more surprising that President Eisenhower has brought to Washington in a conspicuous office one of the most ardent and effective advocates of the Bricker Amendment. Clarence E. Manion, former Dean of the Law School of Notre Dame University, was made chairman of the President's commission on Intergovernmental Relations. This commission, charged with what the President called 'an historic undertaking' and a 'great national purpose' is expected to define the lines of intergovernmental authority and eliminate functions, duplications and waste in federal-state relations.

"Dean Manion takes the extreme States' rights position on the Bricker Amendment, going so far as to indicate his approval of a resolution requiring each of the 48 states to approve a treaty with a foreign power before it would have the force of law in those states. His testimony before a Senate

Judiciary Sub-Committee last April 6 (1953) caused Secretary of State John Foster Dulles acute embarrassment.

"With the purring approval of isolationist-nationalist senators, Manion read from a speech Dulles had made in April of 1952 before a regional meeting of the American Bar Association in Louisville, Kentucky.

"In that speech Dulles stressed the broad treaty-making powers of the President, saying those powers were so sweeping that a treaty could take powers from the states and give them to the federal government or an international body. That was, of course, long before the election of Eisenhower and Dulles' appointment as Secretary of State.

"Manion told the committee that Dulles' statement proved the urgent need for the adoption of the amendment at the earliest possible moment. He said he was distributing hundreds of copies of the Dulles speech wherever he spoke. When he resigned at Notre Dame, Manion was made a special adviser to the National Americanism Commission of the American Legion and he added that he had spoken for the Bricker Amendment to American Legion posts in virtually every state in the Union.

" 'This is the hottest question since the Civil War,' the witness said. 'If the American people know that the Constitution is in danger, they are going to be heard from, and they are beginning to learn about it.'

"Dulles followed Manion before the committee with the statement that the amendment would seriously hamper his work. He was given such a rough time by the same Senators who had eulogized Manion that finally even the diplomatic Dulles came to the end of his patience. He was pressed by Senator Arthur Watkins (R-Utah) to say why the President should have the right to make executive agreements under treaties with foreign governments. Under the treaty signed by the United States and 12 western European powers setting up the North Atlantic Treaty Organization for the defense of the West, up to 10,000 executive agreements have been entered into, Dulles explained.

" 'Do you want all those brought down here?' Dulles finally said as he was badgered by Watkins. 'Every time we open a new privy, we have to have an executive agreement. I take it that that answers it.'

"Manion, in talking to this reporter, said he had not changed his views on the Bricker Amendment. He is speaking about it whenever he is invited to. The chairmanship of the Intergovernmental Commission is only a part time assignment. As chairman, Manion has offices in the Department of Health, Education and Welfare. Secretary Oveta Culp Hobby is one of the governmental members of his commission. Besides the public members and those from the administration, four governors are on the commission, three of whom, Alan Shivers of Texas, Dan Thornton of Colorado and John Battle of Virginia, are all out States'-righters. The fourth member is Governor Alfred E. Driscoll of New Jersey."

Article with a Washington dateline, reprinted from the *Louisville Courier-Journal*, Louisville, Kentucky, Saturday, January 30, 1954, signed by Joseph and Stewart Alsop:

"According to the most responsible White House authorities, the President has decided to ask Dr. Clarence Manion to resign the chairmanship of a special presidential commission on intergovernmental relations. Dr. Manion is to be fired for cause, the cause being his persistent virulent attacks on all opponents of the Bricker Amendment, who of course, include the President himself. . . .

"The President has said that he is going right down the line to beat the Bricker Amendment. Fighting this crucial issue to the finish is in character with the powerful executive leadership which the President has been displaying since the Congressional session opened. But you do not go down the line in politics when you let your friends and supporters be publicly undercut by your own appointees, masquerading as your own chosen experts. . . .

"This is, of course, a dilemma that has confronted the President ever since he took office. The Bricker Amendment fight beautifully sums up the whole problem."

Washington, January 6, 1954 (*Chicago Tribune Press Service*), *Chicago Daily Tribune*, January 7, 1954:

"The pros and cons of treaty law and its impact on internal domestic affairs will be presented at a dinner January 26 (1954) under the auspices of a foundation established to promote wider study and understanding of treaty law, it was announced today.

"Clarence Manion, former Dean of Law at the University of Notre Dame, will present arguments against law by treaty and in favor of such legislation as the Bricker Amendment which says a provision of a treaty which conflicts with the Constitution of the United States shall not be of any force or effect.

"Speaking in opposition to the Amendment which is scheduled for action at this session of Congress, will be Dr. Edward S. Corwin, Professor Emeritus of Princeton University and Secretary of the Committee for Defense of the Constitution by Preserving the Treaty Power."

Human Events, Washington, D.C., January 27, 1954:

"The dinner given Tuesday night, January 26, by the Foundation for the Study of Treaty Law at the Mayflower Hotel was jammed to capacity and the addresses of the speakers were carried over 500 radio stations into every corner of the nation. Most effective was Dean Clarence Manion, who explained the Bricker Amendment, simply, logically and convincingly."

Speech made by Clarence Manion on January 26, (1954) Washington, D.C., in a discussion with Edward S. Corwin of Princeton University at the dinner referred to in the preceding dispatch of January 26 in the *Chicago Tribune* and in *Human Events*, January 27, supra:

"It is impossible to appreciate the necessity for the Bricker Amendment without a sympathetic understanding of the scope and purpose of the American constitutional system as a whole. Constitutional government in the United States is rooted in the self-evident truths of the Declaration of Independence. There, with the first breath of the new life of the Republic, it is stated that government is man's agent for the protection of God's unalienable gifts of life and liberty. For the first time in human history, government was thus logically and categorically reduced from its traditional role of tyrannical mastery to the simple service and deliberate will of human nature. This unprecedented transition is the very essence of the American Revolution. The Founding Fathers knew that government would not surrender its historical pre-eminence without a sustained struggle. All of man's vigilance and all of man's strength would be needed to hold government in its subordinated position of servitude. George Washington summed up their problem in a sentence: 'Government,' he said, 'like fire, is a dangerous servant and a fearful master.' To prevent a renewal of the fearful tyrannical mastery of government the Founding Fathers tied it down with strong chains, namely, checks, balances and divisions of the American constitutional system. They not only proclaimed human liberty, but they defined it in the clear terms of strict constitutional limitations. This is what Woodrow Wilson meant more than 100 years later when he said, 'The history of liberty is the history of the limitation of governmental power.' That history of liberty is as short as the brief history of the United States. Liberty has lived in this country because here, government and every officer, department and division of government has been limited by law. This strict limitation of civil government has been made possible only by the self-government, self-restraint, and moral self-control of the American citizen. The Constitution of the United States was the crowning climax of this determination to use the fire of government effectively but only while it is contained and held firmly in ironclad legal restraints. Thus the Constitution was written to make sure that no officer of government could roam unrestrained over the rights of the American people. It was written precisely to guarantee that Americans would be governed by laws rather than by men. 'In questions of power,' warned Thomas Jefferson, 'let no more be said of confidence in man but bind him down from mischief by the chains of the Constitution.' Perhaps the strongest and most significant links in those constitutional chains are the 9th and 10th Articles of the Federal Bill of Rights in which personal rights and state rights are underscored in these words:

" 'Article 9. The enumeration in the Constitution of certain rights shall not be construed to deny or disparage others retained by the people.'

" 'Article 10. The powers not delegated to the United States by the Constitution nor restricted by it to the States, are reserved to the States respectively or to the people.'

"Now in the 178th year of our liberty and independence, we are apparently come 'full circle.' We discover that there is a handy loose link in these binding constitutional chains: a convenient escape-hatch in this strong wall of constitutional restraints.

"Let Mr. John Foster Dulles tell us about it in his own words, spoken at Louisville, Kentucky, in April, 1952. Said Mr. Dulles:

" 'The treaty-making power is an extraordinary power, liable to abuse. . . . Treaties,' continued Mr. Dulles, 'can take powers away from the Congress and give them to the President. They can take powers from the states and give them to the federal government or to *some international body* and they can cut across the rights given to the people by their Constitutional Bill of Rights.'

"I am sorry to confess that Mr. Dulles' statement is a restrained and accurate description of the treaty power as it is now indicated by court decisions.

"Up to our day and time the treaty power was never used to do any of the things Mr. Dulles describes. Until recently our treaties were contracts between the United States and foreign nations to regulate our foreign affairs. But we are now told by an official State Department document (State Department Publication 3972, Foreign Affairs Policy Series 26, 1950) that 'there is no longer any real difference between domestic and foreign affairs.' It is in this new dispensation of internationalism that treaties are now made. More than 100 of these new-fashioned treaties drawn in the International Labor Organization at Geneva are now pending before or are on their way to the United States Senate for ratification.

"More ominous than this is the scheduled international revision of the United Nations Charter in 1955. In the famous Steel Seizure case (*Youngstown Sheet and Tube Co. v. Sawyer*, 343 U.S. 379, 1952), three Supreme Court Justices were of the opinion that the U.N. Charter and the North Atlantic Pact, as they are now written, justified the Presidential seizure of the steel mills, the Constitution to the contrary notwithstanding. What will the U.N. Charter *not* justify after it has been appropriately strengthened next year?

"Do you want treaties or their often secret counterparts, executive agreements like Yalta or Potsdam, to 'take powers from Congress and give them to the President?' to 'take powers from the states and give them to the federal government or to some international body?' Do you want treaties to 'cut across the rights guaranteed to the people by the Constitution or Bill of Rights?' If you are determined that treaties shall not do these things, then you must support the Bricker Constitutional Amendment which puts treaties under all provisions of the Constitution where treaties belong, rather than on top of and superior to the Constitution where treaties are now.

"What is the Bricker Amendment? You have heard many preposterous statements about it. Let us read it for a change:

" 'Section 1. A provision of a treaty which conflicts with this Constitution shall not be of any force or effect.'

"Is anybody against that? No real American wants a treaty or an executive agreement to set aside all or any part of the Constitution. This section of the Bricker Amendment would seem to be taken by common consent.

" 'Section 2. A treaty shall become effective as internal law in the United States only through legislation which would be valid in the absence of treaty.'

"Let us put a period after the word 'legislation' for a moment. The first sentence would then read: 'A treaty shall become effective as internal law in the United States only through legislation.' This hypothecated sentence merely puts us on a par with other nations of the world with whom we customarily make treaties. As international obligations (for *external, international purposes,* that is) all treaties with all nations are effective upon the nations which ratify them, immediately upon ratification. With the certain exception of Mexico and the possible exception of France, however, the United States is now the only country in the world in which a treaty is self-executing, that is, immediately effective as *domestic internal law* without subsequent legislation. Why should a treaty between the United States and Canada, for instance, immediately and automatically become effective *as the domestic internal law of the United States when it is inoperative and ineffective as the internal domestic law of Canada* until legislation concerning it is passed by the Dominion legislature and, if Provinces are affected, by the Provincial legislatures of Canada? If we thus put a period after the word 'legislation,' this opening sentence of Section 2 merely equalizes our treaty procedure with that of the other nations of the world.

"Now let us read Section 2 straight through as it is written:

" 'A treaty shall become effective as internal law in the United States only through legislation which would be valid in the absence of treaty.' This is the much-discussed 'which clause.' What does it do? It merely prevents the treaty from giving Congress or the state legislature powers which are denied to them in the Constitution of the United States. The 'which clause' prevents a treaty from 'taking powers from the state and giving them to Congress, or to some international body,' such as the General Assembly of the United Nations, for instance, or the International Labor Organization in Geneva. The 'which clause' does not require treaties to be ratified by all of the 48 states, as the opponents of the Amendment have falsely said that it does. As the Constitution is now written, each of the 48 states has reserved control of local domestic affairs such as marriage, divorce, property ownership and public education. The Bricker Amendment would not change this basic reservation of state jurisdiction under the Tenth Amendment, but the Bricker Amendment would prevent the destruction of this basic state jurisdiction, or its transfer to Congress or some international body by a treaty or executive agreement. Neither the 'which clause' nor any section of the Bricker

Amendment 'would hamper the President in his constitutional authority to conduct *foreign affairs*.' It *would* frustrate foreign nations in their attempt to regulate our American domestic internal affairs such as our trials by jury, our free press, our free speech, the free practice of our religion, our free state controlled public and private schools, and our private, unsocialized ownership of property. It would prevent the barter of our traditional bills of rights (which are really bills of prohibitions against governments) in exchange for some international covenant modeled after the Russian Soviet Constitution.

"The 'which clause' would not make it necessary for any state to ratify any treaty. States do not ratify treaties under any circumstances now or under the Bricker Amendment. The 'which clause' would preserve the presently prevailing method of ratification by the Senate of international agreements governing our foreign relations. It would prevent the Constitution from being changed or amended by a treaty so as to deprive the state legislatures or Congress of their respective constitutionally-established legislative powers to regulate the domestic, internal affairs of this country.

"Section 3 of the Bricker Amendment reads:

" 'Congress shall have power to regulate all executive and other agreements with any foreign power or international organization. All such agreements shall be subject to the limitations imposed on treaties by this article.'

"I am confident that Congress has that power now, although many lawyers are skeptical about it. If the courts should ultimately agree with the skeptics, the result would be a complete *carte blanche* of unlimited, untouchable governing power, not for treaties ratified by the Senate, but for the secret agreements made at some future Yalta or Potsdam conference.

"Personally, I am confident that the present administration will never avail itself of this treaty loophole to barter away the constitutional rights of the states or the constitutional rights of the American citizens. But the Bricker Amendment is not being written as a protection against the present administration. The Bill of Rights was not written as a defense against the administration of George Washington, but it has been used to protect the rights of American citizens in thousands of cases since that time. In years to come, when less conscientious administrators, perhaps, are in charge of the government in Washington, thousands of American citizens will likewise rejoice at the protections afforded to them by this proposed Bill of Rights against treaties, because a Bill of Rights against treaties is what the Bricker Amendment actually is.

"Finally, here are some things that the Bricker Amendment would *not* do. It would not affect the wide war powers of Congress or impair the right of Congress fully to regulate foreign and interstate commerce in all things including such items as atomic energy materials and narcotics. It would *not* disturb the President's custody of our *foreign* relations or his broad powers as Commander-in-Chief of our armed forces at home or abroad. The Bricker Amendment would not have prevented the Berlin air-lift, the occupation of Japan and Germany, or the Korean truce.

"But the Bricker Amendment *will* prevent treaties and executive agreements from violating your God-given rights and your constitutionally protected immunities. It will prevent treaties and executive agreements from absconding with the rights and powers reserved to the states of the Union under the Tenth Amendment. Last, but not least, it would safeguard the sovereignty of the United States from subtle and surreptitious larceny by the rabid advocates of world government. In this respect the Bricker Amendment is a renewed declaration of American freedom and American independence. It deserves your active support."

Fort Wayne News Sentinel, Feb. 22, 1954:

"President Eisenhower finally yielded to the insistent clamor of a vicious internationalist cabal, spearheaded by the *New York Times* and the Henry Luce *Time-Life* smear brigade, *Washington Post* and New Deal columnists and has fired Dr. Clarence Manion because of his support of the Bricker Amendment. Abject capitulation of the administration in demanding the resignation of the chairman of the Committee on Intergovernmental Relations, of course, constitutes a signal immediate victory for the internationalists. Ironically, however, Dr. Manion's martyrdom unquestionably will prove to be one of the greatest possible elements of continuing strength for the principles embraced in the Bricker Amendment. . . .

"Consistently enough, the hue and cry that Eisenhower fire Manion was begun last October by the leftist ADA (Americans for Democratic Action), which supported Adlai Stevenson. Planted stories then began appearing in the New Fair Deal press including some by veteran left-winger Marquis Childs who wrote that Manion had been ordered to modify his views on the Bricker Amendment. He retracted when Manion branded it untrue. The pro-State Department *Washington Post* then got into the act with a revival of the ADA attack. The *New York Times* and *Time Magazine* chorused their demands that Manion be fired and New Deal Columnists, Joseph and Stewart Alsop, quoted 'the most responsible White House authorities' as stating that President Eisenhower has 'decided to ask Dr. Manion to resign,' and adding that Manion was to be fired because of his 'persistent virulent attack upon all opponents of the Bricker Amendment, who, of course, include the President himself.' The mouthpieces of the international cabal kept up the pressure on Ike unrelentingly. Finally, to his discredit, he surrendered. But Dr. Manion has the satisfaction of knowing that in firing him, the President unwittingly advanced the principles of the Bricker Amendment immeasurably."

Eisenhower: The Inside Story, by Robert J. Donovan (Harper & Brothers, New York), p. 105:

"When the election was over, Taft was invited to meetings at the Commodore, at which he was treated with great respect. His recommendations for appointments to the Department were received politely by the Eisenhower staff, although only one of them named on Taft's list turned up in the Cabinet. This was Benson. Some of the others, however, were eventually given lesser jobs. For instance, Taft had recommended Clarence E. Manion, former Dean of the Notre Dame Law School, for Attorney General. The post went to Brownell, of course, but Manion was later named chairman of the President's Commission on Intergovernmental Relations. That was one appointment that did not work out well, and in February, 1954, Adams forced Manion to resign. Manion said that he was ousted because he had contravened administration policy by supporting the Bricker Amendment. The fact of the matter was that the White House had its fill of Manion's extreme right-wing views, and the President was dissatisfied with his conduct of the Commission."

The Chicago Tribune, March 13, 1954:

"Clarence E. Manion challenged opponents of the Bricker Amendment, limiting Presidential treaty powers, to answer three questions yesterday.

"The former Dean of Notre Dame University's Law School asserted that he was fired from a governmental position bestowed by President Eisenhower because of speeches favorable to the amendment. Manion spoke at a luncheon meeting of the Executives' Club of Chicago in the Sherman Hotel. 'Why should the President in concert with foreign governments have the power to change the Constitution?' asked Manion.

" 'Why should the President, with the consent of foreign nations, exercise powers over the people and the state which the Constitution forbids the President alone, or the President and Congress together, to exercise?'

"Specifically, just what is it that our diplomats plan to do, which the Bricker Amendment would prevent them from doing? 'The American people are entitled to a frank and immediate answer to these questions,' Manion said, and challenged the members of the club to demand the answer.

"Manion contended that without the Bricker Amendment the President is free to change the Constitution almost at will. Supporters of the Bricker Amendment assert that the constitutional provision which provides that ratified treaties become the supreme law of the land opens the door to a law contrary to the Constitution itself.

" 'If the President can get someone from Guatamala to agree with him, he could rule the country by decree,' said Manion. 'He could take complete command of education, health, labor, highway, and other fields of legislation.'

"Manion asserted that the Bricker Amendment is designed to stop the trend toward centralization of power in the federal government and to revive States' rights. He declared that such centralization of power must be stopped because it is the first step toward the Communist victory in the United States."

PART TWO

☆ AGENDA FOR THE
CONSERVATIVE AMERICAN ☆

Conserve our National Independence
Restore the Constitutional Integrity of the States
Remove the Peril to Private Property
Make the Constitution Enforceable
Liquidate the Menace of Communism

10

The Conservation of American Independence

☆☆☆☆☆

The perpetuation of our national sovereignty is the condition precedent for the accomplishment of every other item on the conservative agenda. This first, most important objective does not imply that the Conservative American is an "isolationist." On the contrary, conservatives are convinced that the last best hope for the ultimate freedom and advancement of men and nations everywhere is a strong, constitutionally governed and nationally independent United States of America. This being so, those Americans who are sincerely concerned with the welfare of all the world must think of America first.

The Communist conquest of mankind is in abeyance now solely because of the actual and potential strength of independent American action. If either our strength or our ultimate unfettered determination to use it can be weakened by our commitments to international organizations, the Communists will have removed the one big road-block that lies between them and their goal of world domination. Whenever our commitments to the United Nations have hampered the independence of our action, as in Korea and Cuba, the Communists have advanced their frontiers dangerously and disastrously for the cause of free men everywhere. If American wealth and will power could ever be completely submerged in some kind—any kind—of international world authority, the hopes for free civilization would soon pass beyond the possibility of redemption.

Under these circumstances it is painful and demoralizing to find the prospects for world peace and international welfare so frequently projected upon proposals for the firm and final abolition of American sovereignty. The snobbish advocates of World Government disdain to discuss the merits of their Utopian objective because these merits are supposed to be taken for granted. A centralized government for all the world is blandly presupposed to be the final burial place for all of the evils that have beset mankind through the ages. On this assumption the goal of World Government becomes so glorious in itself that it justifies any way or means of achieving it, including the frequent misrepresentation of history.

We are told, for instance, that the constitutional consolidation of our own American Republic provides an exact pattern for similar consolidations of nations throughout the world. This perversion of the facts is so gross that conservatives cannot let it pass unchallenged.

When our nation was "conceived in liberty" in 1776, the conception took the form of an official declaration that the nation was composed of "free and independent states." Thirteen years later when the Constitution of the United States was adopted, the new nation was federated into a national union.

The existing independence of the several states then became *the independence of the United States* whose constituent powers were divided between the existing states and the new federal government by the provisions of the Constitution of 1787.

The new federal government with its expressly limited endowment of powers, was created by the people in and for the several states, respectively, *each state group acting separately and independently through conventions called for this purpose in each existing state*. The Constitution provided that it would be established *"between the states so ratifying the same"* when ratification had been accomplished by conventions called for that purpose in at least nine states. The ninth state to ratify and thus technically to put the new Constitution into effect on June 21, 1788, was New Hampshire. Conventions in Virginia and New York followed suit on June 26, 1788 and on July 26, 1788, respectively. The ratifying states chose Presidential electors who met in February, 1789, and voted unanimously to elect George Washington as the first Constitutional President of the United States.

On the ensuing April 30, 1789, Washington was inaugurated and assumed the duties of his new office. At that time the United States consisted of only *eleven* states. North Carolina and Rhode Island had failed to ratify the new Constitution at the time of Washington's inauguration. Their status then, and until the time that each subsequently ratified the Constitution, was that of free, independent and completely sovereign States.[1] If it had been practicable and desirable for either or both of them to do so, they might have retained that sovereign and independent status indefinitely by the simple expedient of continuing to refuse to ratify the Constitution of the United States.

This historical record of its development clearly reveals the peculiar nature of our existing national sovereignty. Between 1776 and 1789, the "United States" was literally a "league of nations." The final ratification of the Articles of Confederation in 1781 did not change the sovereign nature

[1] North Carolina ratified the Constitution November 21, 1789. Rhode Island withheld ratification, until May 29, 1790, and was thus a completely "free and independent state" for more than a year following Washington's first inauguration.

of the "free and independent states," respectively, and that document expressly said so.[2] However, the ratification of the Constitution of 1787 did change the sovereign nature of the constituent states in the particulars and to the extent described in that Constitution. By separate and individual acceptances of the Constitution in 1787, *the people of each state* transferred to the federal government *certain items of sovereign power* that each state had been exercising for itself since the Declaration of Independence. For instance, each of the eighteen specified powers delegated to the Congress of the United States in Article I, Section VIII of the Constitution, had been exercised by each state for itself prior to its ratification of the Constitution. Ratification of the Constitution thus amounted to a subtraction of these and other similarly delegated powers from the reservoir of sovereignty in each state and a consolidation of these subtracted powers in the new Federal container as the sum of the power of the United States government. The states severally were thus left with all of the sovereign powers of government that were not delegated by each of them to the new federal government created by the Constitution of 1787 and made effective for each state by its ratification thereof.[3]

This historical origin of power in our federal government is critically important in view of present proposals and United Nations practices that would effectively transfer items of United States sovereignty to supranational organizations. The steps in the organization of the United States under our present Constitution certainly do not constitute a

[2] Article II of the Articles of Confederation (1777): "Each State retains its sovereignty, freedom and independence, and every power, jurisdiction and right, which is not by this Confederation expressly delegated to the United States, in Congress Assembled."

[3] Constitution of the United States, Amendment X: "The powers not delegated to the United States by the Constitution, nor prohibited by it to the States, are reserved to the States respectively or to the people."

pattern for the consolidation of our Republic with other nations into a world superstate. Nevertheless, our Revolutionary and Constitutional history is frequently cited as an argumentative precedent for further international federations leading eventually to a single government for the entire world.[4]

The method proposed by the World Federalists calls for the accomplishment of such a supranational authority by a multilateral treaty, similar to the United Nations Charter, or

[4] In 1936, Justice Sutherland gave an assist to this misconception of our revolutionary history in the following dictum (*U.S. v. Curtiss-Wright Export Corporation* 299 U.S. 304, 315, 1936):

"The broad statement that the federal government can exercise no powers except those specifically enumerated in the Constitution, and such implied powers as are necessary and proper to carry into effect the enumerated powers, is categorically true only in respect of our internal affairs. In that field the primary purpose of the Constitution was to carve from the general mass of legislative powers then possessed by the states such portions as it was thought desirable to vest in the federal government, leaving those not included in the enumeration still in the states. (*Carter v. Carter Co.* 298 U.S. 238, 294) . . .

"It results that the investment of the federal government with the powers of external sovereignty did not depend upon the affirmative grants of the Constitution. The powers to declare and wage war, to conclude peace, to make treaties, to maintain diplomatic relations with other sovereignties, if they had never been mentioned in the Constitution, would have vested in the federal government as necessary concomitants of nationalisty."

The broad assumptions in the above quotation are directly contrary to the facts of our history. The sweeping summation in the last sentence is effectively rebutted by the simple question: What was the status of Rhode Island and North Carolina respectively with reference to these powers between the time that Washington was first inaugurated and the date when each of these states subsequently ratified the Constitution of the United States? While *Missouri v. Holland* (252 U.S. 416, 1920) and *United States v. Pink,* (315 U.S. 203 1942) are generally cited as the chief offenders in giving treaties and Executive Agreements a supraconstitutional status (see the discussion of the Bricker Amendment, supra, p. 105) the above-quoted language, if accepted as true and controlling, would clearly destroy the last vestiges of the federal system of carefully balanced powers that the Founding Fathers labored so arduously to contrive, ordain and finally establish between the time of the Stamp Act (1765) and the ratification of the Constitution in 1789.

by a Convention of Nations to draw a Constitution for World Government either of which would be effective when ratified by the respective nations. On its face the second alternative seems to fit the precedent established here in 1787-1789, but the analogy falls apart in the historical analysis of the federation of the United States.

By the language of our Constitution and as a matter of historical fact evidenced by the experience of North Carolina and Rhode Island,[5] the several states of the Union have retained all of the incidents of sovereign nations that were not delegated to the federal government in the Constitution. The several states did *not* give the federal government the power to re-delegate any of the powers that they deposited with it, to a supranational body, nor did they give the federal government the authority to subordinate the reserved powers of the states respectively to any international alliance or organization. To follow the American precedent of 1787-1789 in the formation of a World Government, it would be necessary to submit the proposed new international Constitution *to conventions in each state,* called for the purpose of considering the proposal with the power in *each of the several states of the United States* to accept the international Constitution or to reject it and remain in "status quo." This is what was done in the case of the Constitution of 1787. A ratification of a proposed international Constitution by resolution of Congress, or by the Senate, if such Constitution were submitted as a treaty, would certainly not conform to the precedent established in the ratification of our Constitution, nor to the letter and spirit of the Constitution itself.

But there are practical as well as historical and constitutional considerations that call for the careful conservation of our national independence. Responding to the inspiration of personal freedom and individual initiative, the people of the

5 See footnote 1, supra.

United States have developed and accumulated more than fifty per cent of the productive resources of the world and this, if you please, with only six per cent of the total world population. Any scheme for a "democratic" international organization of the world would put these American resources at the mercy of a predatory population pool in which we would be outnumbered at the rate of 16 to 1.

The first move of the new international "democratic" parliament would be to "share the wealth" of the United States among the populous "have-not" nations which could and undoubtedly would thus vote themselves into temporary affluence. In a disarmed world where the omnipotent central government alone would wield effective military power, we would have no alternative but to submit to this new-style international "due process of law."

It is vain to expect that any superstate—world-wide or regional in its authority—could be restricted to the exercise of a few limited powers. By its very nature, centralized power is dynamic and aggressive. All of its forces are centripetal. In the vortex of an authority that is supreme in one area, it is next to impossible to maintain respect for the diffusive principle of subsidiarity in and for any area. *Sooner or later a World Government of one thing would become a World Government of everything.*

Here again, the history of our own Federated Republic is revealing and awesome. In spite of the crystal-clear mandate of the Tenth Article of the Bill of Rights,[6] there is now no item or area of sovereign jurisdiction that the several States of the Union can call their very own.

American history reveals that a prime ingredient of central power is the principle of expansion which is characterized by

[6] "The powers not delegated to the United States by the Constitution, nor prohibited by it to the States, are reserved to the States respectively, or to the people."

its steadily increasing acceleration. Its slow start at the beginning of the United States was disarming and deceptive. When Washington was first inaugurated, Alexander Hamilton and others feared that the central government might soon succumb to the disintegrating influence of established state sovereignty. Nevertheless, slowly but surely and with ever-increasing speed the centripetal force of the central power principle asserted itself in the ever-expanding influence of the federal establishment.

In the course of his campaign for the Presidency in 1912, Woodrow Wilson warned that "a concentration of governmental power is what always precedes the death of human liberty." In retrospect, and in the context of 1912 conditions, Wilson's warning was merely prophetic. Looking upon it now, concentrated governmental power in the United States was conspicuous by its absence in 1912. However, in the years between then and now we have seen the greatest concentration of power in the federal government that has ever taken place on earth *with the consent of the people over whom the power of government was to be exercised.*

This was no tyranny imposed suddenly and ruthlessly by the iron hand of an invading conqueror. On the contrary, the American people asked for it—or were made to believe that they did—in contrived doses of "federal aid" that developed an insatiable popular appetite for more and more of the same. Today, the very concentration of power against which Woodrow Wilson warned us has actually taken place. At the present time, the President of the United States holds more power over the liberty and property of more people than can be found in the hands of any government official on earth outside of the heavy impenetrable curtain of Communism. There is very little that has been done to the people of Cuba by Castro that could not now be done to the American people by our President if he possessed the will to do such things and lacked the impeding restraints of his moral conscience. It is quite true that this terrible conclusion is refuted by whole pages and paragraphs of our Constitution, but the fact is that for all practical purposes these constitutional restraints are no longer enforceable against the President and/or his federal agents and agencies.[7]

In spite of thundering denunciations against the "wrongs" of King George III that appear in our Declaration of Independence, it is now a settled determination of American courts that the ancient dictum, "The King can do no Wrong"

[7] In modern times, the only case ever prosecuted successfully to resist arbitrary action by the President of the United States involved President Truman's seizure of the steel mills in 1952. (*Youngstown Sheet and Tube Company v. Sawyer*, 343 U.S. 376.) Difficulties encountered by mill owners in this classic attempt to recover their property are described in "The Anatomy of a Constitutional Law Case" by Alan F. Westin, (Macmillan & Co., New York, 1958). When the case reached the Supreme Court, nine of the Justices produced seven separate opinions and the consensus of legal and constitutional principle, if any, upon which the decision was rendered, is next to impossible to discern. The nose count of the Supreme Court Justices was six to three against the seizure. Whether the decision went against the President, the United States, or against Charles Sawyer as an individual, who as Secretary of Commerce, was charged with the execution of the Presidential Order, is not entirely clear, but owners did succeed in repossessing their property. The government's defense was based upon the power of the President to do as he pleased with the property and persons of the people in any grave emergency. This position was made clear when the proceeding was before the Federal District Court. At that time the judge asked the government lawyer this question:

"When the sovereign people adopted the Constitution, it enumerated the powers set up in the Constitution. . . . limited the powers of the Congress and limited the powers of the Judiciary, *but it did not limit the powers of the Executive. Is that what you say?*"

Mr. Baldridge, for the government, answered:

"That is the way we read Article II of the Constitution." "The Anatomy of a Constitutional Law Case, supra. p. 64.)

The three dissenting Justices agreed with the government's position. *If two more of the nine Justices had agreed with the dissenters, the position of the government concerning the unchallengeable omnipotence of the President would have been affirmed. In the Steel Seizure Case, therefore, the country found itself just two Supreme Court Justices away from despotism.*

applies also to our federal government. The result is that the United States government cannot be sued, or enjoined, or otherwise affirmatively "brought to book" in court, unless it has previously given its consent to the action.[8]

---

8 In civil and criminal proceedings brought by the federal government against individuals, it is still possible for accused persons to defend themselves by alleging that the involved statute, order, citation or method of its enforcement violates specified provisions of the federal Constitution. As a defense, such allegations will be considered by the Court on their merits and in the recently sensitized area of civil rights, the chances of success, particularly in criminal cases, are better than even. But the Constitution was not intended to serve merely as a shield for the relatively few people who are formally accused in civil and criminal court actions. This use of the Constitution is simply an important by-product of its main purpose, which was to construct a hard and fast confinement for the expressly limited checked and balanced powers which the Constitution confers upon the federal government. When the federal government, through the activities of its officers and agents, steps over any of the sidelines marked out for it in "the Supreme Law of the Land," it commits a trespass upon the areas reserved to the several states and/or to the American people. At that point it should be subject to suit in the same manner and through the same kind of proceedings that are available against ordinary trespassers who violate the laws protecting the privacy, property and liberty of the people generally. In ordinary cases, the remedy for such trespass is affirmative and immediate. The trespasser is not asked to "give his consent" to a suit against him for a palpable violation of the law. He is served with a summons and required to defend the action against him or be defaulted. If such offenders were required to "consent" to such litigation, the involved law against trespass would be reduced to a dead letter. But this is precisely the situation in cases of trespasses committed by the federal government where the law alleged to be violated is the *Supreme Law of the Land*. The "sovereign immunity" doctrine thus enables the federal government to do as it pleases, constitutional restrictions and restraints to the contrary notwithstanding. The "consent" of the government to be sued is sharply qualified in the consentual statutes and strictly construed by the Courts. In the Tucker Act (1887) Congress established a blanket consent for the United States to be sued in cases involving contract claims by individuals or corporations, and permitted such suits to be brought in the several District Courts as well as in the Court of Claims. The Federal Tort Claims Act (1946) gave another blanket waiver of the "sovereign immunity doctrine" in cases where individuals or corporations, suffering damage from the negligence or malfeasance of government agents, may recover their damages, with certain

United States history has thus expanded the famous dictum of Lord Acton into something like this: *Power corrupts and by its nature tends to become absolute.* This is precisely what Woodrow Wilson was talking about in 1912, namely, that personal liberty can be protected only when and where the centralization of power is impossible.

But the Wilsonian warning was sounded long before Woodrow Wilson was born. George Washington had more to do with the establishment of our unique American Republic than any other person. Our distinguished first President was no political doctrinaire. He was first and foremost a practical patriot who recognized that the powerless central government established by the Articles of Confederation was worse than useless, because its existence on paper created the popular illusion of a united security among the several states, which in fact did not exist. It was Washington who promoted the Philadelphia Convention of 1787 and prompted it to pro-

---

limitations as to the amount of damages suffered. But the exceptions written into that Act are impressive.

Examples of the results of such exceptions to the "consent" under the Tort Claims Act can be found in such cases as the following:

Bell v. Hood, 71 Fed. Supp. 813 (1947), where the government was not liable for the unlawful search by one of its agents acting within the scope of his authority.

Denahey v. Isbrandtsen Co., 80 Fed. Supp. 180, (1948), where the government was not liable for false imprisonment resulting from the official acts of its agent.

Gubbins v. U.S., 192 Fed. 2d 411 (1951), where the government was not liable for damages for a libel committed by its agent in the course of his official duty.

Coates v. U.S. 181 Fed. 2d 816 (1950), where the government was not responsible for damages resulting from a discretionary act of its agent. See also *Dalehite v. U.S.* 346 U.S. 15, (1953).

It is possible to sue and recover against an officer of the government, but only for his private acts that are unrelated to his official duties. The government may not be sued under the guise of a suit against one of its officials. (*Malone v. Bowdoin,* 369 U.S. 643, (1962); *Larson v. Domestic and Foreign Commerce Corporation,* 337 U.S. 682 (1949).

duce a new Constitution rather than a series of amendments to the existing Articles of Confederation. But impressed as he undoubtedly was with the necessity for adequate government as insurance against the agonies of anarchy, Washington was not deceived about the insidious nature of government itself. "Government," he said, "is not reason, it is not eloquence, it is force; like fire, government is a *troublesome servant and a fearful master. Never for a moment should it be left to irresponsible action.*" [9]

The Constitution of the United States reflected the general distrust of the "fire of government" that prevailed during the formative years of the United States. Only small "fires" can be effectively controlled and the spread and jointure of these several fires of government into a destructive conflagration of tyranny can be prevented only by constant vigilance and the highly skilled labor involved in balancing one segment of fire against another, by fighting fire with fire, in other words.

The popular controls that are necessary to guard government against "irresponsible action" are inherently weakened in the proportion and to the extent that such controls are removed from the ready reach of the people who must exercise them. A world government would be so far removed from the control of anybody except its self-perpetuating bureaucracy that it would quickly become a completely irresponsible despotism. If it is next to impossible now to protect personal rights against unconstitutional violation by our own federal government, what hope could there be for the successful assertion of personal liberty against the foreign agents of a World Government? [10]

In the ideal community, the personal, morally-directed

9 *Dictionary of Similes,* by Wilstach (Little Brown & Co., Boston), p. 526.
10 See note 7, supra.

self-government of each person should be enough to generate the common good of all.[11]

But in practice this ideal order burdens each individual with a maximum of responsibility which very few of us are willing to assume and execute. There is an innate urge in our "tainted nature" which pushes away the responsibility that each of us has a moral obligation to embrace and discharge. "Let George do it" is an epigrammatic summation of the modern tendency to "pass the buck" of personal responsibility to somebody else. If "George" is unwilling to pick up the check, some branch of government is nominated to do so. This recourse is a comforting sedative for the pangs of personal conscience because in America "the government is us" and when we pass personal obligations on to the government we are, as it were, fulfilling our personal duty, although vicariously.

But such an obligation, once removed merely, is not far enough away. The miscarriages of the township, city and county governments are too obvious to be ignored. Official

[11] "It must be remembered that ninety-five per cent of the peace, order and welfare existing in human society is always produced by the conscientious practice of man to man justice and person to person charity. When any part of this important domain of personal virtue is transferred to government, that part is automatically released from the restraints of morality and put into the area of conscienceless coercion. The field of personal responsibility is thus reduced at the same time and to the same extent that the boundaries of irresponsibility are enlarged. Expansion of the governmental domain in this manner is unfortunate for two reasons. The first is purely practical: Government cannot manage these fields of human welfare with the justice, economy and effectiveness that is possible when these same fields are the direct responsibility of morally sensitive human beings. *This loss of justice, economy and effectiveness is increased in the proportion that such governmental management is centralized.* The second reason is basic: Any shrinkage in the area of personal responsibility tends to frustrate the purpose for which man was created. Man is here to be tested for his free compliance with the moral law of God. A great part of this law concerns man's relationships with man " *The Key to Peace*, by Clarence Manion, (The Heritage Foundation, Inc. 1950) pp. 36, 37.

mistakes at these local levels of authority are constantly being brought back to us for correction through personal attention and personal political action. Deputations of responsibility to adjacent local authorities always carry reversionary clauses which put the problems back into the very laps from which they were evicted.

The urge to escape responsibility then proceeds to rationalize the advantages of bigger, more remote, more centralized "and therefore better qualified" administration of the troublesome problems. This is the cue for the state or federal government to move in and take over, after which there is a consequential relaxation of pressure upon the conscience of the local community. The blunders and the blunderers are now comfortably out of sight. When a national scandal brings them back into the local newspaper headlines, the average citizen salves his conscience with the pious, patient acknowledgment that he is powerless to do anything about it. At this point the original sin of personal irresponsibility has come full circle and personal liberty is ready for a total and permanent eclipse.

The nervous system for the execution of all of this public responsibility, local, state and federal, is tax revenue. When the building of a new high school will add one cent to the local property tax rate, every taxpayer in the township is put upon notice to see that he gets his money's worth. A new federal building in the same neighborhood may cost each of these people twice as much in taxes, but that calculation is lost somewhere on the long round trip that his money takes to Washington and back.[12] Consequently, while he gripes

12 "The Tax Foundation has calculated that on the basis of 1962 figures, five out of every six federal aid dollars go back to the states in which they were originally collected. That's a conservative calculation. . . . The 1962 aid programs totaled roughly $7,600,000,000. Yet of that huge total only about $800,000,000 actually was moved from richer states to poorer states. . . . There's a tremendous amount of waste motion in taking dollars to Washing-

about the high school, the taxpayer cheers the new federal installation as a gift from Santa Claus.

For the people who raise and spend public money, the moral is written in large capital letters, namely: *Keep the authority to raise the money and the power to spend it as far away from their sources—the people—as possible.* For the implementation of this basic bureaucratic principle, the city is better than the township; the metropolitan region is better than the city; the state is better than any of its subdivisions and the federal government is far and away better than any other tax-collecting, tax-spending entity in the country. By the same token, direct taxes and spending by the United Nations or a full-fledged World Government would suit bureaucratic purposes even better.

If you think it is difficult to get a specified public accounting of what the federal government spends for any of its projects—and it is very difficult to obtain that—try and imagine, for instance, just how you would proceed to find out what the United Nations Organizations is spending to assist the Communist enemies of the United States. The clerk who embezzles $500.00 in the office of the County Treasurer is practically sure to be caught, punished and pilloried before the

---

ton and then carrying them back where they came from. . . . For instance, Indiana citizens pay out in taxes to supply the money, $1.44 for every $1.00 that comes back in aid. . . . Federal aid is misnamed. Five-sixths of it is not aid at all. It is just money taken out of the taxpayer's pocket and then handed back to him with a grand gesture, as if it were from Santa Claus. This five-sixths is control money. It causes states and localities to inaugurate or continue activities which they otherwise would not choose to carry out. Or it causes them to operate activities in ways or on a scale different from what they otherwise would do. *It governs the spending by states of their own money.* Almost every federal grant program requires some matching percentage of state or local funds. The federal administrators set the rules for spending this money. If a spade were called a spade these would be labeled federal control programs. That's what they are."
Indianapolis Star editorial, May 15, 1963.

local community in short order. Contrast this with the situation uncovered by a Congressional Committee which investigated our Foreign Aid distribution in just one country, namely Iran:

"The so-called expanded technical assistance program which began in January, 1952, and resulted in United States obligations of over 100 million dollars in a 5-year period . . . was undertaken without such basic requirements of prudent management as adequate controls and procedures, with the inevitable consequences that *it is now impossible to tell what became of these funds.*"
(The Director of the Iranian Foreign Aid mission was subsequently promoted.)

> *United States Aid Operations in Iran,* House of Representatives Committee on Operations, January 3, 1957.

The cure for the chronic ills of the world will not be found in more centralization of governmental authority. On the contrary, the remedy for many of these disturbances lies in *the radical de-centralization of the governmental authorities now existing.*

A vindication of this basic principle of conservatism requires that the massive, ideologically-interlocked Communist empire, now ruling the lives of a billion people, be broken up into the historic pattern of self-governing, nationally independent components that are presently merged into helplessness by the ruthless force of the Communist conquest. In like manner the gratuitous and growing assertions of authority by the United Nations must be retracted into the positive limitations spelled out for that organization in the United Nations Charter. Failing such retreat and retraction, the Conservative American would get the United States out of the United Nations completely.

Our slavish support of the United Nations' illegal interferences in the domestic affairs of independent nations has made us an accessory to crimes committed against our own allies in the cold war and turned over the management of our foreign policy to the direction of the United Nations General Assembly—a revolutionary body that now runs the United Nations in defiance of its charter.[13] The American people would have reversed this disreputable United States policy long ago but for the sustained stream of official, professionally-directed propaganda that sanctifies the United Nations and all of its works as the only alternative to a nuclear holocaust.

The flexibility of this brainwashing flood of what is repre-

13 The United States contributes about one-third of the general U.N. budget, and about 40% to 70% of the U.N. Special Fund. During the past five years the United States has donated one hundred million dollars to the Special Fund and nearly two hundred million dollars to the Expanded Technical Assistance Program since 1951. From these funds the U.N. is supporting such projects as furnishing radioactive isotopes to Yugoslavia, Communist textbooks for Cuban school children, training airmen and servicing airplanes in Mexico for Cuba, providing a fishery study for Castro to improve the Cuban fishing fleet that may also be useful in running guns to Central America, sixteen separate U.N. financing projects in Cuba, and many U.N.-associated agencies such as the International Labor Organization, the International Atomic Energy Agency, UNESCO, the Food and Agriculture Organization and others. The United States paid up to 70% of the total cost for the Congo operation where we successfully defeated the anti-Communist Tshombe in Katanga and installed the pro-Communist government in the Congo. Financial aid is still being furnished to the Congolese government. We have paid for solving Red Poland's farm problems and have furnished industrial knowledge with war potential for both Poland and Yugoslavia. Soviet Russia has refused to contribute any money for some of these United Nations enterprises on the ground that the General Assembly has no authority under the U.N. Charter to undertake them. For once, the Kremlin is on firm legal ground.

sented as "fact and truth" is both frightening and effective. The convincing current turns alternately from the appeasement, conciliation and therefore the aggrandizement of Communist power to the call for increased authority and exclusive military forces for the United Nations, but invariably it waters down and washes out popular sentiment for the national sovereign independence of the United States.

A popular vision of endless international peace is kept floating in this propaganda flood upon the myth of "world law" administered by an omniscient "World Court." We are thus led to assume that both of these great resources of justice are now completely established and waiting to function fully for everybody everywhere when and if the United States brings itself to tap these available resources whole-heartedly and without reservation.

The fact is, of course, that there is no such thing as "world law" and what is euphemistically called the "World Court" is merely a nondescript board of arbitration which is precluded from functioning serviceably as such because of the permanent membership of two Communist members on its fifteen-man panel of "judges." There is no "world law" now for the simple reason that there is at present no world parliament constituted to make such law for the world in the same manner that Congress is constituted to make law for the United States.

In the establishment of a government of and by law, whether it is for a local community, for a state or for the world, the first essential step is the adoption of a Constitution which creates in the following order: (a) a legislature to make the laws; (b) an executive to enforce the laws passed by the legislature; (c) courts to judge infractions of the laws in actions brought by the executive or by private citizens.[14] Thus a "court" properly so-called can exist only as the logical

14 See Articles I, II and III, Constitution of the United States.

consequence of the legislative and executive branches of the government for which the court functions. Without a legislature and an executive, a "court" such as the present World Court, can arbitrate factual disputes that are submitted to it from time to time by the voluntary agreement of the disputants, but it has no "law" to apply nor is any law "made" by its decisions.

In spite of this obvious fact, the tub-thumpers for "World Peace through World Law" campaign lustily for complete compulsory jurisdiction for the World Court over all disputes arising between any and all members of the United Nations.[15] Our adherence to the World Court Statute (1946) was made with expressed reservations, to which the so-called Connally Amendment was added on the Senate floor before the Treaty was ratified. The Connally Amendment made it explicit that we would be the judges of what constituted domestic questions which we withheld from the jurisdiction of the World Court. "As determined by the United States," says the Connally Amendment. If these six words were knocked out of our act of adherence to the World Court Statute, the court would thereby and thereafter be empowered to make its own independent and final determination of whether or not a dispute brought before it is a "domestic" concern of the United States.[16]

15 See Senate Res. 166 introduced by Senator Russell Long, Louisiana, June 20, 1963.

16 " 'As determined by the United States'—six little words, but what a symbol they have become! To many they are a symbol of an unrealistic approach to modern international affairs. To as many others they are just the opposite— a symbol of the realistic safeguarding of our vital interests during a cold war. These six words have divided families and friends. They have split the lawyers of the country into two opposing camps. Although the issue transcends party lines, the 1960 platform of the Democratic party called for repeal of the Connally Amendment. And yet, in that same year when the Senate was considering the matter of repeal, its members were deluged by the petitions of hundreds of thousands of citizens who fervently opposed such action. . . .

With the Connally Amendment, the decision as to what is or is not a domestic issue of this country is made by this country.

Without the Connally Amendment, our continued control over our immigration and/or tariff policies would be questionable, to say the least. There would be very little question about our continued right to make our own decisions concerning the Panama Canal, Puerto Rico, and our Guantánamo Naval base in Cuba. These vital and vested domestic interests of the United States would henceforth be submitted to the tender mercies of the World Court.

In spite of this ominous prospect the abolition of the Connally Amendment is the immediate objective of that articulate and influential group of internationalists who are determined to destroy American sovereignty. These people realize that abolition of the now famous "six little words" would be a long and important step toward the complete abandonment of our national independence.

Justification for our national independence as the predicate for local self-government ends where it begins, namely, in "the Laws of Nature and of Nature's God." The one common denominator of all the races of men on earth is the continuing responsibility of each person to his Creator. Permanent improvement in human civilization can be brought about only by sharpening that sense of personal responsibility in all men everywhere. The greatest political agency for the propagation and protection of this saving principle of truth is

---

The retention of the Connally Amendment—the guarding of our national sovereignty ourselves rather than placing it in the hands of the World Court for safe keeping—is essential to the ultimate victory of freedom in the present struggle."

Too Grave a Risk—the Connally Amendment Issue, by Denison Kitchell, (William Morrow and Company, New York, 1963), pp. 18, 126.

This is an excellent analysis of the "World Peace Through World Law" fantasy.

the self-conscious strength of the independent, constitutionally governed United States of America. This nation was founded upon the self-evident truth that men are created with a God-imbued duty to govern themselves. Propelled by this principle, our politically organized society has moved forward faster in freedom than any nation in the history of the world. To wreck this solid accomplishment in an attempt to construct a new international Tower of Babel would be an act of wanton vandalism. The Conservative American is determined to prevent it.

T he powers not delegated to the United States by the Constitution, nor restricted by it to the States, are reserved to the States respectively, or to the people."

The above quotation is the final article of what we know as "the Bill of Rights." This "bill," which comprises the first ten amendments to the Constitution, was proposed by the Congress at its first session, September 25, 1789. Virginia, the eleventh state (there then being fourteen in all) ratified this Bill of Rights on December 15, 1791.

The point to observe and remember is that these ten amendments were considered by the Congress and ratified by the states as a single piece of Constitutional reform. Here was a balanced program for the insured protection of private personal rights against violation by the federal government. For this unitary purpose and to this single end the Tenth Amendment was and is just as important as the First Amendment, and/or all or any of those in between.

Acting for and by himself, the individual citizen would frequently be incapable of fending off an invasion of his rights by federal agents. For practical purposes it is often necessary for the citizen to have recourse to state power in such a personal defensive effort. As a matter of law and in point of fact, he must link his defense with the reserved power of the state in the area of authority where the threat to his liberty is made by the federal government. By the same token when his state attempts an unauthorized exercise of power over his person or property, the citizen can and does defend himself frequently by claiming that jurisdiction over the involved transaction has been given to the federal government by the Constitution of the United States. In other words, the constitutional division of powers between the states and the federal government is an important part of the main constitutional purpose which is to protect the inalienable liberty of the individual citizen. In many instances, personal protection can be achieved only by balancing the constitutional power of the state against that of the federal government and vice versa.

We have become accustomed to the expression "States' rights." This is an acceptable phrase to denote the reserved area of state authority, but strictly speaking it is inaccurate. Only persons have "rights." In the United States "powers" are given to government so that it may protect the "rights" of the people. The framers of the Constitution made this clear in the Tenth Amendment which, as a part of the Bill of Rights, refers to "powers" of the states.

The Ninth Amendment is likewise specific:

"The enumeration in the Constitution of certain *rights* shall not be construed to deny or disparage others retained by the *people*." (Italics added.)

The reason for federal power and for state power is the same, namely, the need for protection for personal rights which owe their existence to the laws of nature and of nature's God. Neither the Bill of Rights nor the Constitution as a whole "creates" or "grants" any personal rights. Our Constitutions, state and federal, are merely a co-ordinated mechanism for the protection of personal rights against violation by any branch of this government or by anybody else.

This postulate which is basic to the understanding and application of our American constitutional system, is confused by such expressions as "civil rights" and "civil liberties." "Civil rights" is a misleading designation for privileges created by state or federal law. Such federal "privileges" are comparatively few in number for the reason that under the Constitution the great bulk of governing power over the people is left in the area of state authority. Federal privileges include such things as the opportunity to go through bankruptcy, to get a passport for foreign travel, and to sue in a federal court. State privileges include the "right" to vote, to drive an automobile, to send your child to a public school, and hundreds of other such licenses that are the creatures of state laws.

Strictly speaking, there is no such thing as a "civil liberty." To say that something is "civil" is to imply that it is the creature of the "civil government." Liberty is not in that category. In the American constitutional dispensation, liberty is a gift of God which it is the duty of government to protect. To call God-given liberty "civil" is to degrade it and to suggest that its sanction is exclusively secular and material which of course it is not.

The responsibility of each person in the management of his own liberty and the menace of centralized governmental power to the proper execution of that responsibility has been treated elsewhere in this book.[1] The Founding Fathers were certainly not thinking about the menace of Communism when they co-ordinated our federal system of government, but they obviously had the menace of centralized power in mind, and Communism is precisely such a menace with all of the attributes of ruthless materialistic amorality added to it.

1 P. 140 et seq., supra.

The history of the Communist conquest has shown that Communism cannot be established in any place unless and until the governmental authority over that place is completely centralized and made absolute. On the other hand, when all the levers of power have been conveniently brought together and consolidated, the big Red hand soon closes over the consolidation and human freedom immediately disappears.

Thus, unconsciously perhaps, but nevertheless certainly, the Founding Fathers of our constitutional system built into it an impregnable defense against a Communist inside takeover of this country which they nailed down and riveted into place by the unmistakable language of the Tenth Amendment.

Among the powers "not delegated to the United States," for instance, are these:

(a) The control of local police forces
(b) The control of voting and elections
(c) The control of private property ownership
(d) The control of public education
(e) The control of public communication[2]

In every country that the Communists have taken from the inside (and they have taken all of them that way, beginning with Soviet Russia) each of the controls listed above was in the hands of certain "ministries" of a central government. By forcing their agents into these strategic offices through "coalition governments," the Communists clamped down upon the police first and upon the other vital areas very rapidly thereafter, usually in the order listed above.[3]

[2] Speech and the Press. See Amendment I.

[3] The post-World War II history of Czechoslovakia provides a revealing example of the vulnerability of a centralized government to this Communist tactic of infiltration and take-over. Czechoslovakia was an advanced industrialized country with an exceptionally high standard of living and a democratic constitution. Nevertheless, it fell into complete Communist control as quickly

The reserved powers of the states over these and other vital areas of American life is the best form of insurance against the success of a Communist "putsch" in the United States. With elections, property ownership and the police firmly and exclusively controlled by fifty separate state governments, the effect of Communist penetration of our federal government could be effectively neutralized until the American people would be able to recover the lost ground through political action. For instance, unless and until the Tenth Amendment is torn to shreds it would be impossible for any Communist official in our federal government to expropriate private property, as was done by a decree of the Central Government in Czechoslovakia in 1945. In that same country, at the time of the May, 1946, elections, the Communist Ministry of the "Interior" stationed Communist policemen at the ballot boxes as a form of intimidation. The scheme worked and the Communists won a majority of seats in the Czechoslovakian Parliament. This was the last "free" election held in that unhappy country.

In view of the effective and perfidious use Communism has made of centralized power during the past thirty years, the importance of the Tenth Amendment to the continuity of American freedom would appear to be self-evident. Nevertheless, it is painful to observe that the advance of the Communist conquest throughout the world has almost exactly paralleled the official, progressive destruction of state power within the United States. The apathetic indifference of the American people to the important relationship between "States' rights" and their personal liberty has been reflected in a long line of decisions by the United States Supreme Court. These Court constructions have now reached the

---

and as easily as any country of eastern Europe. See *And Not a Shot is Fired. The Communist Strategy for Subverting a Representative Government*, by Jan Kozak, (The Long House, New Canaan, Conn.)

point where the Bill of Rights is regarded as a bill of prohibitions against state regulations in the very area of authority reserved to state government by the terms of the Tenth Amendment. While it is practically impossible successfully to challenge, much less effectively to restrain, the everexpanding power of the federal government,[4] state laws, processes and regulations are continually being nullified by decisions of the Supreme Court of the United States. In certain of its conclusions involving state legislation, the Court has retained the instant cases on its docket as a means of monitoring the subject matter of the law suit administratively.[5]

In 1958, thirty-six state chief justices joined in a remonstrance against the United States Supreme Court for "raising considerable doubt" that we still have "a government of laws and not of men." The state judges said:

"It is strange indeed to reflect that under a Constitution which provides for a system of checks and balances and of distribution of powers between national and state governments, one branch of our government—the Supreme Court—should attain the immense and in many respects the dominant power which it now wields. . . . We do not believe that either the framers of the original Constitution or the possibly less gifted draftsmen of the Fourteenth Amendment ever contemplated that the Supreme

---

[4] See Chapter 10, note 8. Chapter 13 supra.

[5] *Brown v. Board of Education of Topeka,* 347 U.S. 483, (1954).
The Court in the Brown case "retained jurisdiction" by ordering that the case be restored to the Court's docket and requesting the parties to present further argument on two principal questions involved in the case: whether a decree of the Court should order immediate integration, or gradual integration, and whether the Court should formulate detailed decrees governing enforcement of its decision or whether the Court should remand the case to the local courts with directions to frame specific decrees.
Baker v. Carr, 369 U.S. 186, (1962), which ordered the Tennessee legislature to reapportion.

Court would, or should, have the almost unlimited policy-making powers which it now exercises." [6]

The validity of this criticism is quickly revealed by an examination of the Supreme Court's decisions concerning religion and the public schools. At this stage, the Court's language is snarled in an involved effort to describe the kind of "establishment of religion" that was comprehended by the First Amendment. The controlling fact that the Amendment in term and intent restricts "Congress" and is not directed at state action has been buried since 1948 under the Court's gratuitous assumption that the First Amendment, in all of its terms, is blanketed into the Fourteenth Amendment as a restriction upon state action.[7] From that time forward the Supreme Court has been construing the phrase, "Congress shall make no law respecting an establishment of religion" as if it read, "No state shall make any law, etc." In none of the "prayer cases" from then to now has the Supreme Court or anyone representing the parties before it, sought to question or reverse this primary error which has produced all of the hue and cry about Church and State—God and the government, etc.—that has shocked the moral sensibilities of the American people. What the First Amendment explicitly affirmed was the exclusive power of the several states to deal with the subject of religion without interference by the federal government. The control of religion, like education, the press, agriculture and other such things, was among those "powers not delegated to the United States" by the Constitution, and therefore "reserved to the States respectively." The Fourteenth Amendment was not designed to change this fundamental division of jurisdiction, and for seventy years after

[6] *U.S. News and World Report,* Oct. 3, 1958, p. 92 et seq.
[7] *State of Illinois ex rel. McCollum v. Board of Education,* 92 L. Ed. 649, (1948).

the Fourteenth Amendment was adopted, no Supreme Court decision ever held that it was so designed.[8]

In the process of destroying the vitality of the Tenth Amendment, the Supreme Court has been burning the states' candle at both ends. With the Court's approbation, Congress may now regulate anything anywhere that "affects" interstate commerce. Under the Court's definitions and descriptions of when and how such commerce is "affected," the area of exclusive state control shrinks out of sight.[9] During the same period the Court has held that Congress may regulate whatever it subsidizes,[10] and since it is impossible for either a state or a taxpayer to question the constitutionality of a congressional appropriation, Congress may bring any subject within its regulatory jurisdiction by the simple expedient of voting a subsidy for it.[11]

Unfortunately, the vital importance of the Tenth Amendment is heavily clouded now by sectionalism and the hot-tempered controversy over segregation. Let it be assumed for sake of argument that some states have and may continue to use their constitutionally reserved powers in a manner that

---

[8] See *"The Church, The State and Mrs. McCollum,"* by Clarence Manion, *Notre Dame Lawyer*, Vol. 23, p. 456.

[9] U.S. v. Darby. 85 L. ed. 609, (1941).
"I have not yet adequately expressed the more than anxiety that I feel at the ever-increasing scope given to the Fourteenth Amendment in cutting down what I believe to be the Constitutional rights of the States. As the decisions now stand, I see hardly any limit but the sky to the invalidating of those rights if they so happen to strike a majority of the Court as for any reason undesirable. I cannot believe that the Amendment was intended to give us carte blanche to embody our economic or moral beliefs in its prohibitions. . . . We ought to remember the great caution shown by the Constitution in limiting the power of the States, and should be slow to construe the clause in the 14th Amendment as committing to the Court, with no guide but the court's own discretion, the validity of whatever laws the states may pass."
(Justice Holmes in *Baldwin v. Missouri*, 281 U.S. 586, 595, 1930.)

[10] *Wickard v. Filburn*, 87 L. ed. 122, 1942.

[11] *Frothingham v. Mellon*, 67 L. ed. 1078, 1923.

displeases or even shocks citizens of other states. This was and is to be expected. If it had been contemplated that all states would use their reserved powers in every case in exactly the same way, the Tenth Amendment would have been without value or purpose. It was the fact that the several states had and would continue to have local problems that were peculiar to their geography, as well as to their religious, social and political traditions, that made the Tenth Amendment a necessary prerequisite to orderly government within "a more perfect union." The Constitution would not have been ratified except for the promise of its advocates that the First Congress would propose to amend it by a Bill of Rights for the explicit protection of personal liberty and reserved state power.[12]

People generally, and the Justices of the Supreme Court of the United States particularly, need to realize that the Tenth Article of the Bill of Rights is no less important to the maintenance of liberty and to the continuity of our national life than the First Article. Public apathy and popular misconception have encouraged the Supreme Court to ignore both precedent and principle in the development of a judicial pattern for the systematic destruction of Constitutional

12 "Several States ratified only after Washington put forward the suggestion that the desired guarantees could be added by amendment." *The Constitution of the United States*, Edward S. Corwin, Editor, (Government Printing Office, 1953,) p. 750.

"At the first session of the First Congress, Madison introduced the first ten amendments to the Constitution and against much opposition, induced the House to decide in favor of their submission to the States for ratification. He recognized that powerful forces throughout the country were insisting that Congress should go further and call a second Convention to revise the Constitution and he thus sought to avert the great danger to the Constitution and to his own political future if Congress trifled with the popular demand for amendments." (*The Constitution of the United States*, James M. Beck. George H. Doran Company, 1924, p. 192.)

state power.[13] Today, when all the forces of science, technology and communications are centripetal, *essential* personal liberty, personal responsibility and local self-government can be preserved only by a maximum of continuous resistance to the ever-accelerated drive for complete centralization of power. If the Supreme Court continues to be an incorrigible adjunct in this over-all centralistic process which is destroying the constitutional integrity of the States of the Union, then Congress should suspend the Court's appellate jurisdiction as Congress has the constitutional power to do and thus leave appeals on federal constitutional questions in the final determination of the respective federal Circuit Courts of Appeal.[14] If this appears to be an heroic recourse, he who hesitates to use it needs only to remember that the constitutional division of power between our states and the federal government is the warp and woof of our liberty-protecting constitutional system. If this division is permitted to be discredited in any manner for any reason, all permanent value

[13] "It has long, however, been my opinion, and I have never shrunk from its expression . . . that the germ of dissolution of our federal government is in the constitution of the federal judiciary; an irresponsible body, (for impeachment is scarcely a scare-crow,) working like gravity by night and by day, gaining a little today and a little tomorrow, and advancing its noiseless step like a thief, over the field of jurisdiction, until all shall be usurped from the States, and the government of all be consolidated into one. To this I am opposed; because when all government, domestic and foreign, in little as in great things, shall be drawn to Washington as the centre of all power, it will render powerless the checks provided of one government on another and will become as venal and oppressive as the government from which we separated." Thomas Jefferson, Letter Aug. 18, 1821, to Charles Hammond. See *Jefferson's Writings,* Vol. XV, pp. 330 et seq.

[14] Article III, sec. 2, United States Constitution: "In all cases affecting ambassadors, other public ministers, and consuls, and those in which a state shall be party, the Supreme Court shall have original jurisdiction. In all other cases before mentioned, *the Supreme Court shall have appellate jurisdiction* both as to law and fact, *with such exceptions and under such regulations as the Congress shall make.*"

will then and there be drained from what is left of our constitutional system. Nothing worth preserving will remain. On the resulting ruin and for the protection of his liberty, the Conservative American will have to start to build all over again.[15]

[15] "If the day should ever arrive (which God forbid) when the people of the different parts of our country should allow their local affairs to be administered by prefects sent from Washington, and when the self-government of the States shall have been so far lost as that of the departments of France or even so far as that of the counties of England, on that day the progressive political career of the American people will have come to an end, and the hopes that have been built upon it for the future happiness and prosperity of mankind will be wrecked forever."

Written in 1885 by John Fiske in *The Critical Period of American History*.

12

The Peril to Private Property

☆☆☆☆☆

"The theory of the Communists may be summed up in the single sentence: *Abolition of Private Property.*" [1]

In its essence the Communist conquest is a world-wide war against privacy. When and if the Communists win this war, every door and window will be wide open to continuous surveillance by "Big Brother." As long as the privacy of any person, place or thing is officially respected, the Red victory will be incomplete.

Under Communism private property is abolished precisely because private property provides insulation for personal privacy and for some degree of personal independence, neither of which can be tolerated under the absolute authority of the ruling dictatorship. Complete Communist victory will thus establish the ultimate in dehumanized materialism. Such an environment is so directly at variance with the God-given nature of man that the average free person is incapable of comprehending the full horror of complete Communist control.

Some conception of what happens to the human spirit when privacy is abolished is provided in George Orwell's

[1] *Communist Manifesto.*

novel, *1984,* and particularly in the author's accounts of the "telescreen," which in *1984* is everywhere.

The telescreen received and transmitted simultaneously. Winston Smith, the harried "hero" of Orwell's book, was always sure of the fact that:

"Within the field of vision which the metal plaque commanded, he could be seen as well as heard. There was, of course, no way of knowing whether you were being watched at any given moment. . . . It was even conceivable that *they watched everybody all the time.* You had to live . . . in the assumption that every sound you made was overheard, and, except in darkness, every movement scrutinized." [2]

The telescreen, like everything else, including the walls of the rooms to which it was affixed, was public property. Any interference with its emplacement would thus be a high crime against the state. Nevertheless, this all-seeing eye, all-hearing ear, and ever-available voice, was merely one instrument in the vast complex of continuous scrutiny which the dictatorship found it necessary to employ in order to enforce the conscienceless coercion of its centralized materialistic rule.

The tortured way of life described in *1984* explains why the encouragement and maintenance of private property ownership is a continuing form of insurance against the establishment of Communism. It was with calculated deliberation that Marx and Engels, in the Communist Manifesto, summed up the objectives of the Communists in five words, namely, *The Abolition of Private Property.*

By the same token, those who now oppose the Communist conquest of mankind might be expected to sum up their program of resistance to Communism in an equally short and simple sentence, namely, *The Protection of Private Prop-*

2 *1984,* by George Orwell, (Harcourt, Brace and Co., New York, 1949), p. 4.

erty. However, the people who look for this kind of simple, uncomplicated logic in the anti-Communist program of the United States government today are doomed to disappointment and dismay.

By and large, our modern politicians have lost all contact with the hard realities of human life and human liberty that went into the foundations of our Republic. The framers of our constitutional system knew nothing about Communism as such, but they clearly understood the nature of man and they were well aware of the indispensable concomitants of human freedom. In our Constitutions, state and federal, they welded "life, liberty and property" together on a basis of continuing mutuality for the equal protection of all three. "Due process of law" at every level was marshaled into a solemn protective device against arbitrary attacks upon this trinitarian concept that encircles the broad base of human rights. Our constitutional law was made to run forward and back through "life, liberty and property" without pause or priority until they became one and inseparable.

This primary principle of our constitutional system is now lost upon those who govern the United States. On the floor of Congress or elsewhere, it is a commonplace for ignorant demagogues to expand upon the "priority of personal rights over property rights" and to stress a distinction where in fact and law there is none. As we have seen, all "rights" are "personal." [3] The right legitimately to acquire, own, hold and transmit property, like the right to life and liberty, is a personal right inherent in the nature of man. Consequently, there is no such thing as a "property right." Those who degrade what they ignorantly call "property rights" are undermining the integrity of the very human personality that they profess to exalt and protect. What is worse, they are removing the basic barricade between that personality and its

[3] Chapter 10 supra.

complete submergence by the Communist conquest. At no point has the conservation of our basic resources been more flagrantly violated than here.

Marx and Engels knew very well that the only way to abolish private property is to convert it into public property. They also knew that when all private property has become public property, the people will likewise have been made public. They spelled out their plan to bring this about in the following language:

"The proletariat [the dictatorship] will use its political supremacy to wrest, by degrees, all capital from the bourgeoisie [private property owners], to centralize all instruments of production in the hands of the State. . . . Of course, in the beginning, this cannot be effected except by means of despotic inroads on the rights of property, and on the conditions of bourgeois production by means of measures, therefore, which appear economically insufficient and untenable, but which in the course of the movement, outstrip themselves, necessitate further inroads upon the old social order, and are unavoidable as a means of entirely revolutionizing the mode of production." [4]

For many years now our government has slavishly followed this prescription for the eventual establishment of the Marxian social order. Socialist influence upon our official action is now so strongly placed that all, or nearly all, of the major bills pending before Congress at any time will be found to impinge in some manner upon the private management of private property. The federal government has used and is still using four broad approaches to the final point where all private property will be made public, namely, *taxation, regulation, appropriation* and *direct operation of* private property and production. At different times and places one or

[4] Communist Manifesto, p. 42.

more of these roads will be found to cross or merge with another, but their direction never changes and they all lead inexorably to the same place.

It is inconceivable, of course, that this rapid socialistic development which, as Marx prophesied, is "entirely revolutionizing the mode of production" could be happening by accident or as a response merely to the "democratic" forces of political gravitation. On the contrary, the development is competently managed. It has a co-ordinated literature and a tireless and dedicated academic "élite" which has pushed hard for its progress for more than thirty years. In and out of the classroom, on and off the public payroll, those apologists for "Democratic Socialism" have managed to put the free enterprise for private profit system on the defensive and keep it there. It was this Socialistic school, preaching and implementing the doctrines of the English economist, John Maynard Keynes, that made "a New Deal" out of the first administration of Franklin D. Roosevelt and thus scrapped the orthodox, private enterprise platform upon which Roosevelt ran and was elected in 1932.[5]

[5] See Chapter 2.

The establishment of Keynesian principle in government circles has been so thorough that even non-socialists and anti-socialists have been compelled to carry out Keynesian policies. Harvard's J. Kenneth Galbraith gloats over the fact of a government in the Keynesian pattern.

"There is a widespread notion that one of the most primitive of modern ideological choices is whether a government shall be Keynesian or not. . . . No present or future administration really has the non-Keynesian choice."
Economics in the Art of Controversy, 1955. pp. 100-101.

Keynesian leftists, while holding power under New Deal and Fair Deal administrations, constructed bureaucracies (manned by swarms of bureaucrats under civil service protection) which operate as self-socialized forms moving leftward regardless of the desires of the electorate or elected officials. They are confident that a great national debt and continuing inflation, plus enormous internal and foreign commitments assure the continuance of Keynesian operations for generations to come, regardless of who is in power. The only alterna-

Once having grasped the political initiative in 1933, our "Democratic-Socialists" have never let it get away from them. Depression, inflation, war, peace and finally the cold war against Communism, have all been used as grist for the big Socialist mill which unremittingly for thirty years has been steadily turning our private property into public property. The resulting loss by what Keynesian J. Kenneth Galbraith has called the "private sector" to the "public sector" of our economy is literally immeasurable, but some indices are available. They indicate the progress and steady acceleration of the drive to "wrest by degrees all capital from the bourgeoisie (and) to centralize all instruments of production in the hands of the State."

For instance, in fiscal year 1951, from its operation of federal business enterprises, the federal government collected in gross receipts, seven billion ninety-four and three-tenths million dollars as compared with two billion, eight hundred and twenty-six million dollars in 1940, and with fifteen billion, seven hundred and ninety-four million dollars for 1963. For these years and for all the years in between, the government operation resulted in an annual loss ranging from one billion and forty-three million in 1940 to four billion, ninety-two million in 1963.[6]

The National Committee for Economic Freedom[7] has distributed an alphabetical descriptive list of more than 700 business-type enterprises that are now owned and operated

---

tive to Keynesism would be some very drastic political surgery, accompanied by a re-organization and abolishment of the greatest part of the federal bureaus.

Keynes at Harvard, (Revised Edition, 1962, p. 77. Veritas Foundation, New York.)

[6] Annual, *Facts and Figures,* (Tax Foundation, 50 Rockefeller Plaza, New York) p. 1940 et seq.

[7] 6413 Franklin Avenue, Los Angeles 28, California.

by the federal government. The annual gross receipts of these commercial activities are included in the figures cited above. All of these operations are competing with privately-owned and privately-operated enterprises. None of these government-owned operations pays any federal, state and/or local taxes, and all of them operate at a loss. These annual losses (more than four billion dollars in 1963) are automatically added to the federal debt and immediately the annual interest on such debt increases become an additional burden upon taxpaying privately-owned enterprises, including those with which these government operations directly compete.[8]

The steady increase in this "public sector" of our economy and the proportionate shrinkage of what remains of the "private sector" constantly builds up the tax burden that is borne exclusively by the property, enterprise and production that remain in private hands. This rapid ever-accelerated progress down the road to complete public ownership is swiftly approaching the critical "point of no return." A progressively diminished area, known as the private property for private profit sector cannot forever pay the deficits for a tax-free, perpetually burgeoning, publicly-owned and publicly-operated sector. Unless this "Democratic-Socialist" drive is promptly reversed, the time will soon come when

[8] The electric utility generating industry presents a graphic case in point. Generating capacity owned and operated by government agencies and government-subsidized co-operatives grew from 6.8% of the total national capacity in 1932 to 24.3% in 1961. At this writing, Secretary of the Interior Udall has announced a plan to create a government monopoly in the long-distance transmission of electric power under the control of his department. To be sure that plans of private power companies to co-operate with each other in the construction of such lines under private tax-paying ownership would not materialize, the Secretary has decreed that no private rights of way would be granted over federal land without his approval. Since half the land in the West is federally-owned, this decree has stymied private plans for transmission lines in that area.

the private property for private profit area must throw in the sponge and surrender unconditionally to the Marxian Socialists who have been working tirelessly at the task of "entirely revolutionizing the mode of production." The fact that most of our private enterprisers are oblivious of this approaching deadline for their compulsive capitulation will not serve to postpone its arrival or soften its revolutionary impact upon their accustomed way of life.

Unfortunately, American businessmen share the prevailing ignorance and apathy concerning this deliberated degeneration of our private enterprise system. This popular indifference is almost entirely responsible for the swift and steady advance of the Socialist program in this country. Many of those who cheer the loudest when the "public sector" is periodically enlarged are naïvely unaware of where the movement is headed.

While the dedicated Marxists who direct this "Democratic-Socialist" drive are keenly aware of its ultimate destination, the semi-Socialists, neo-Keynesians, liberals, do-gooders and welfare-staters, who propel it with a jet-stream of propaganda, are undoubtedly convinced that they can "tax and tax, spend and spend, elect and elect" forever without killing the private enterprise goose that lays the golden eggs.

Meanwhile, however, in the glib political vocabulary of the Socialist cheering section, "profit" is a bad word, representing something somewhat less than respectable. This, in spite of the fact that profits are the source of the federal spending programs that constitute the warp and woof of all that the Democratic-Socialists do and plan to do, here and all over the world. Every year the United States Treasury collects more than one hundred billion dollars in various kinds of taxes levied directly or indirectly upon the profits of private property enterprises. If this source of tax revenue should suddenly dry up, our lavish government programs at home and abroad would soon disintegrate and disappear. Nevertheless we find that our government now fights its supporting private property, private profit system with far greater energy than it employs fighting Communism. The subsidization of Socialism all over the world has been the guiding principle of our government-to-government Foreign Aid program for more than fifteen years. To an ever-increasing degree, Communist governments are being made eligible for the foreign aid money that is sweated out of the profits of American private enterprise.[9] At the same time, our government is disinterested when foreign governments—even those who are the recipients of its foreign aid—confiscate the property of American citizens.[10]

It is significant that the United States government is now insisting upon "agrarian reform" as a condition precedent for its grants-of-aid to governments of Latin America. This is an official invitation to confiscation and socialization of real property in the involved countries. It will be remembered that when the Communists first appeared in Russia, China and Cuba, they professed to be "peaceful agrarian reformers"

[9] Aid to Yugoslavia, 1946 to 1963, totals $2,400,000,000.

Aid to Poland during the same period totals $522,000,000.

Congressional Record, July 15, 1963, p. 11859.

[10] Brazil: $1.9 billion in foreign aid, is now on the brink of Communism. On February 16, 1962, the governor of the State of Rio Grande do Sul, Brazil, expropriated the American-owned telephone system valued at $8 million. February 17, 1962, the U.S. State Department "disapproved" of the seizure *but recognized Brazil's right to expropriate American property.*

(*Congressional Record,* July 15, 1963.)

Venezuela: 214 million in foreign aid. American property destroyed and expropriated without protest.

Cuba: 52 million in foreign aid. Now a Communist Soviet satellite. One billion dollars worth of American-owned property confiscated without audible protest by American government.

—nothing more.[11] "Land, bread and peace" were all they professed to be looking for.

Public ownership of land is a basic objective of the Communist conquest. The reason is obvious. In this country, as elsewhere, all of the "real" property is land. Literally and figuratively, real estate underlies and supports all other forms of property. When the ownership of all land passes completely and without reservation to the government, Socialism will then be an accomplished fact.

At the present time 32.3 per cent of the land and water area in the fifty states is now owned by the federal government.[12] This extensive federal land ownership is not something that we inherited from the Louisiana Purchase. On the contrary, more than one-sixth of this present total has been acquired by the federal government since 1945. Upon one political pretext or another additional acres are constantly being added to this big tax-exempt federal domain.

An important practical consequence of this pervasive pattern of federal ownership is the fact that, on the average, almost one acre out of every three in the country is now exempt from state and local property taxation because it is owned by the federal government. This big exempted area automatically increases the local property taxes on the remaining acreage under private ownership by more than 30 per cent. Thus every additional acre of private land acquired

[11] "The idea that the Chinese Communists were 'peaceful agrarian reformers' was peddled everywhere. In Washington (1945) it became increasingly popular in certain sections of the Department of State. The American press carried the 'agrarian' theme far and wide. Everybody who was 'in the know' was ready to say that the Chinese Communists were entirely different from the Communists of Soviet Russia and would be neither anti-American nor puppets of the Kremlin."

How the Far East was Lost, by Anthony Kubek, (Henry Regnery Co. Chicago, 1963), p. 238.

[12] *U.S. Government Organization Manual,* 1959-60.

by the federal government for any purpose has the immediate effect of raising the local property tax rate on privately owned land in the area where the new federal land ownership is acquired.

Local property tax rates of ten per cent and over are becoming the rule rather than the exception now, and such confiscatory assessments amount to a capital levy which puts private ownership on a short ten-year depreciation tenure. Ten per cent per year is more than the average land owner can clear from the operation of his property before federal income taxes, and unless he can manage to lower the assessed valuation by negotiation or by law, his retreat from land ownership will soon become an economic necessity.

When high local property tax rates have reached and passed the point of diminishing returns to the local taxcollecting government, federal aid looms as the only solution for meeting local government costs for such things as schools, police, streets and public welfare. Since the federal government may, and promptly does, regulate what it subsidizes,[13] such appeals for federal assistance amount to the complete abdication, by local and state governments, of their constitutionally reserved responsibilities.

When the over-all operations of the Federal government are viewed in perspective, this Federal "aid" to the local property tax squeeze shows up as a swindle which aggravates the problem it promises to solve. For if it is continued, Federal Aid will destroy all localized government. In the short run, as we have seen in Chapter 10,[14] federal aid accomplishes federal control over areas otherwise inaccessible to the Washington bureaucracy. Thus, at the present time, it is the most effective agency for the very centralization of power which is a condition precedent to the full establishment of the "proletarian

13 *Wickard v. Filburn,* 317 U.S. 111, 1942.
14 Pp. 17-18.

dictatorship." [15] But beyond that, federal aid helps to bring about the destruction of the private property ownership that is only apparently relieved from confiscatory local taxes by this federal subsidy.

Basically, the source of all federal and state revenue is the same, namely, the private property and personal enterprise of the American people. Every dollar spent by the state or federal government is thus subtracted from the store of privately owned property and to this extent reduces the water in the well to which both governments must subsequently come to quench the thirst for future public expenditures. This being so, federal aid may be likened to a blood transfusion from one part of the body to another part of the same body through a badly leaking tube. If the body is big enough, there may be some immediate relief for a painful localized congestion, but the dangerous consequences to general health from this loss of blood are obvious.

When more public money is being spent than the tax-supplying private property can support in the full stride of private enterprise there is no alternative, short of eventual confiscation and socialism, to a sharp reduction of public expenditures. Every attempt to by-pass this hard economic fact of life and liberty through inflation, debt or otherwise, will amount to compliance with the Marxian directive for wresting capital from the bourgeoisie and centralizing the instruments of production in the hands of the state.

The administrators of our federal fiscal policy lost all contact with this basic principle in 1933 and have been trav-

15 The progress of this centralized power can be measured by the annual increases in federal aid funds through the years to state and local governments: 1949—$1,802,700,000; 1954—$2,657,000,000; 1961—$7,283,400,000; 1962 —$8,680,000,000; 1963—$9,896,600,000.

Facts and Figures, (Tax Foundation, 1962-63), p. 95 supra.

eling down the road to public ownership ever since. On this road, public expenditures, debt, taxes and inflation have been racing with each other for thirty years.

The increased population of the country provides no excuse for the meteoric rise in federal expenditures. In 1934 the federal government spent $47 for every person in the United States. By 1960, the per capita expenditure had increased to $549. Thus in 26 years the growth of federal expenditures was $502 per person faster than the growth of our population. But by 1962 federal expenditures per capita had risen to $613, or $64 per person more than they were in 1960.[16] The curve is still rising. It is obvious that the much advertised population explosion is being muted by the much louder explosion in the federal budget.

But taxing, spending and direct competition are not the only flails that the federal government is using upon our private property for private profit system. The sharp cutting edges are reserved for use by those federal officials who administer the regulations, restrictions, inspections and reporting requirements with which every American private business, large or small, is being tortured today. Listen, for instance, to the president of the Standard Oil Company of Indiana:

"Specters haunt American business today; the manifold and proliferating regulatory agencies of the federal government. The all-pervasive powers and activities of these agencies whose existence was not contemplated by our Constitution, go largely unrealized by the average citizen. . . . Starting in 1887 with the creation of the Interstate Commerce Commission, there has been a step-by-step development of a *fourth* branch of government. Today it embraces over 60 independent agencies with approximately 400,-000 employees and a total budget of around ten billion dollars.

16 *Facts and Figures* (Tax Foundation 1962-63), supra.

We have now arrived at the point at which the eye of some almighty regulatory agency is upon us when we buy or sell, ship or receive, hire or fire, grow or manufacture, save or spend, drink or diet, profit or lose, talk or listen. . . . Moreover, because of the frequent lack of clearly defined areas of jurisdiction between the regulatory bodies, there is widespread confusion as to precisely what a business man or a corporation properly can or should do, as to what body has legitimate authority to make and enforce decisions regarding such conduct, and as to where one can effectively turn for appeal from a questioned ruling."

After citing a specific interference by the government with his own company's sales practices which it took seventeen years and two trips to the Supreme Court of the United States to remove, the speaker concluded:

"This is the kind of thing that can give any responsible business man nightmares at high noon. And it is little more than a taste of what lies ahead unless the course of events can somehow be changed. . . . Unless the trend toward more and more regulation can be halted, it is questionable whether American business can retain the necessary freedom to meet these challenges." [17]

How many small business men could afford two trips to the Supreme Court and seventeen years of exposure to the contingent liabilities involved in order to vindicate their right to compete for the profits upon which federal income taxes depend? The answer is that not one in ten thousand would be willing and able to do what the Standard Oil Company of Indiana did. By and large, therefore, American private enterprise is being conducted precariously and by the grace of federal agents who swarm over the land like the lice of Egypt. Businessmen can only keep their fingers crossed and hope for the best. Commerce is no longer governed by

[17] John E. Swearingen, *The Readers Digest*, August, 1962.

ascertainable law but by the whims of bureaucrats who make their own ground rules to suit each case.

A member of the Federal Trade Commission has said:

"If we had the money, we could get a 'cease and desist' order against every businessman in the United States who is engaged in interstate commerce. The business man has nothing to say. He can only hope that the law of averages will keep him off the wrong end of a complaint." [18]

Every experienced lawyer knows that what the commissioner has said is true and that consequently it is practically impossible to steer a business client through the existing thicket of governmental regulations without exposing him to subsequent reprisals, investigations and possible fine and/or imprisonment by the federal government. The only law upon which the business man can rely today is the Statute of Limitations.

At the very time when "full employment" is being advertised as the prime objective of governmental policy, every person who gives another person a job is automatically saddled with a raft of perplexing and onerous governmental regulations, restrictions and requirements. Civil and criminal penalties are prescribed for the neglect or violation of any one of these. When and if the government's inspectors are finally satisfied, the employer finds himself confronted with legally protected labor union monopolies enforcing compulsory unionism, the dues check-off and industry-wide bargaining. If he quits business, the employer may be held guilty of an unfair labor practice and be ordered to renew his operations with full back pay to all of his idled workers.[19]

[18] Lowell B. Mason, quoted in *Ten Thousand Commandments—A Story of the Anti-Trust Laws,* by Harold Fleming (Prentice-Hall & Co., New York), p. 7.
[19] *N.L.R.B. v. Rapid Bindery Inc.,* 293 Fed. 2d 170, 1961.

The burden of calculating, withholding and remitting the billions of dollars in federal income and Social Security taxes exacted from salaries and wages of American workers each year is dumped upon their employers. If this money is not so collected and sent by the employer to the government in regular installments, months in advance of the date when the taxes are due, automatic fines are imposed upon the employer by the Treasury Department. The entire enormous expense of this drudgery is borne by the employers— the Thirteenth Amendment to the Constitution to the contrary notwithstanding.

"Abolition of property in land" and "a heavy *progressive* and *graduated* income tax" were the first and second steps recommended in the Communist Manifesto for any country that is to be headed down the road to Socialism. We are upon official notice therefore as to where we are going. The penetrative vision of the income tax collectors now is only slightly less ubiquitous than Orwell's telescreen. There are no private personal secrets that may be shielded from routine summary searches by the Internal Revenue servants. For these inquisitors there is no "closed season" and every person in the land is fair game to be snared "at sight."

For the special convenience of these Marxian messengers, the Fourth Article of the Federal Bill of Rights has been effectively repealed. The victim who refers seriously to that archaic protection for personal privacy is automatically in contempt of court.

Some years ago, the chief of all of the federal income tax collectors, Mr. T. Coleman Andrews, who was then called the commissioner of Internal Revenue was so revolted at the "police state methods" frozen into the procedures of income tax collection that he resigned his post and launched a campaign for a public awakening to the dangers that the Income

Tax Law posed to our heritage of freedom. Here is some of what he said at the time:

"On February 4, 1953, I became Commissioner of Internal Revenue. I had always had serious misgivings about the Income Tax Law and not a few suspicions about the manner in which it had been administered. After two years and nine months, I returned to private life at the end of October, 1955, with both my misgivings and my suspicions confirmed.

"Congress (in implementing the Sixteenth Amendment) went beyond merely enacting an income tax law and repealed Article IV of the Bill of Rights, by empowering the tax collector to do the very things from which that Article says we were to be secure. It opened up our homes, our papers and our effects to the prying eyes of government agents and set the stage for searches of our books and vaults and for inquiries into our private affairs whenever the tax men might decide, even though there might not be any justification beyond mere cynical suspicion.

"The income tax is bad because it has robbed you and me of the guarantee of privacy and the respect for our property that were given to us in Article IV of the Bill of Rights. This invasion is absolute and complete as far as the amount of tax that can be assessed is concerned. *Please remember that under the Sixteenth Amendment* Congress can take 100% of our income any time it wants to. As a matter of fact right now it is imposing a tax as high as 91%. This is downright confiscation and cannot be defended on any other grounds.

"The income tax is bad because it was conceived in class hatred, is an instrument of vengeance and plays right into the hands of the Communists. It employs the vicious Communist principle of taking from each according to his accumulation of the fruits of his labor and giving to others according to their needs, regardless of whether those needs are the result of indolence or lack of pride, self-respect, personal dignity or other attributes of men.

"The income tax is fulfilling the Marxist prophecy that the surest way to destroy a capitalist society is by "steeply graduated" taxes on income and heavy levies upon the estates of people when they die.

"As matters now stand, if our children make the most of their capabilities and training they will have to give most of it to the tax collector and so become slaves of the government. *People cannot pull themselves up by their own boot straps any more because the tax collector gets the boots and the straps as well.*

"The income tax is bad because it is oppressive to all and discriminates particularly against those people who prove themselves most adept at keeping the wheels of business turning and creating maximum employment and a high standard of living for their fellow men. . . .

"I believe that a better way to raise revenue not only can be found but *must* be found because I am convinced that the present system is leading us right back to the very tyranny from which those, who established this land of freedom, risked their lives, their fortunes and their sacred honor to forever free themselves. . . ." [20]

What the Sixteenth Amendment has amounted to in effect is a new plenary power in Congress to ignore all of the other constitutional restrictions upon federal power. Due Process of Law and Equal Protection of the Laws must both step aside to let the assessment and collection of the "progressive and graduated" income tax step unchallenged into the lives and fortunes of the American people. Involuntary and unpaid servitude—abolished by the Thirteenth Amendment—is imposed upon every employer with the pains and penalties herein before referred to. The time-honored legal obligation of the creditor to prove his claim against the debtor is

[20] *Income Tax—Speedway to Tyranny,* Manion Forum Radio Network, Broadcast 89, June 10, 1956.

reversed in the case of the income taxcollector. On the contrary, the burden is upon the taxpayer to prove that the arbitrary assessment of the tax and/or penalty against him is invalid.

The Conservative American is convinced that constitutional government cannot be restored while the Sixteenth Amendment is intact. The present right of Congress to authorize the confiscation of any part or all of the income of the citizen using calculated discrimination, with malice toward some and charity for none, in any manner and by any procedure that any federal agent may at any time and place deem expedient, is incompatible with the time-honored traditions of American liberty.

The year 1913 is the traditional "base period" used by economists for measuring the abnormalities that have worked their way into farm price parity and the value of the American dollar. The Income Tax Amendment was added to our Constitution in 1913. Its impact upon our economic system and upon our constitutional law, along with its responsibility for the Socialistic course of our subsequent history, needs to be measured, evaluated and corrected. One author has called the Sixteenth Amendment, "The Root of all Evil." [21] His proof of this thesis is impressive. But root, stem or branch, the fact is now notorious that our Federal Income Tax is an integral part of the Evil Tree of Communism.[22]

Our progressive graduated income tax has imperiled personal privacy and private property, the basic insulation of human freedom. As T. Coleman Andrews has said, "a better way to raise revenue not only can but must be found."

[21] *The Income Tax: Root of All Evil,* by Frank Chodorov (The Devin-Adair Co., New York, 1954).
[22] *An Evil Tree—The Story of Communism,* by Agnes Murphy, (Bruce Co., Milwaukee, Wisconsin, 1961).

At the same time a way can and must be found to drive the federal government out of its growing competition with private enterprise and to destroy its unconstitutional appetite for the destruction of private property. For the accomplishment of this objective, six state legislatures have called for the adoption of a "Liberty Amendment" to the Constitution. Thirty-six additional state legislatures have placed the same proposal on their agenda for action. The time has now come for its consideration by the Congress of the United States.

Here is the proposed Liberty Amendment which the Conservative American will support:

Section 1. The Government of the United States shall not engage in any business, professional, commercial, financial or industrial enterprise except as specified in the Constitution.

Section 2. The constitution or laws of any state, or the laws of the United States, shall not be subject to the terms of any foreign or domestic agreement which would abrogate this amendment.

Section 3. The activities of the United States government which violate the intent and purposes of this amendment shall, within a period of three years from the date of the ratification of this amendment, be liquidated and the properties and facilities affected shall be sold.

Section 4. Three years after the ratification of this amendment the sixteenth article of amendment to the Constitution of the United States shall stand repealed and thereafter Congress shall not levy taxes on personal incomes, estates and/or gifts.

13

Our Unenforced Constitution

☆☆☆☆☆

LOST: The Constitution of the United States.

FINDER: Will please return it to the American people.

REWARD: Freedom.

This advertisement should now be placed in all American newspapers and remain there. The Constitution of the United States has disappeared. The sooner the news is spread and an appropriate alarm is sounded, the better the chance for the recovery of our constitutional government.

But meanwhile, of course, the empty forms of our constitutional procedure will be respected and appropriately venerated. Unbeknownst to practically everybody but themselves, Presidential electors will continue to meet every Leap Year in December and legally elect, as President and Vice-President of the United States, the two men whom the American people have firmly and blissfully, but nevertheless erroneously, believed that they themselves elected on the first Tuesday after the first Monday in the preceding November.

This, however, is a minor misconception. More egregious errors will happen in the succeeding January when the new

President and Vice-President along with members of the House of Representatives and some newly elected members of the Senate will take the oath to support the Constitution of the United States. From that day forward, little or nothing will be said or done about the Constitution of the United States. What the Supreme Court will talk about from time to time as the Constitution will be something else again which has been fashioned out of the Court's own peculiar and accumulated misconstructions.

When he begins his work at the White House, the new President will have sworn: "That I will faithfully execute the office of President of the United States and will, to the best of my ability, preserve, protect and defend the Constitution of the United States." (Article 2, Section 1, United States Constitution.) Under oath he will thus have acknowledged the fact that the office of President was created to preserve the Constitution which describes and limits the powers and activities of the federal government.

After this solemn acknowledgment, the new President will gratuitously assume the obligation of taking care of everybody everywhere on earth.

If the federal government had been designed to do everything for everybody everywhere, the Constitution would never have been written and our Presidents would swear merely to do all things possible for all people.

Immediately after his inaugural oath in 1961, President Kennedy reminded us that "the same revolutionary beliefs for which our forebears fought are still at issue around the world," namely, "the belief that the rights of man come not from the generosity of the State but from the hand of God."

To secure these rights, as our Declaration of Independence says, our new American government was instituted in 1776, and to hold this government on the narrow line of that protective purpose, our Constitution was adopted in 1789. This is the government-restricting Constitution that the President is pledged to support. But, under prevailing circumstances, it is extremely difficult for any President to keep the solemn promise that he has sworn before God and his countrymen to observe.

Many of the continuing and most ambitious commitments of the Presidential office, both to the American people and to the people of the world, have been built up through recent years with a palpable disregard for constitutional prohibitions. This being so, any resemblance between what our Presidents do and what they have sworn to do is purely coincidental.

The President's office is not the only offender against constitutional commandments. Congress and the federal courts are equally guilty and this in spite of the fact that, like the President, every congressman and every federal judge, as a condition of admission to his high office, has sworn to preserve and obey the Constitution of the United States.

When you read the Constitution you will find that it is filled with expressed and implied prohibitions, interdictions and restrictions upon governmental action. Quite obviously, therefore, the Constitution was constructed to limit, divide and distribute the always dangerous but nevertheless necessary powers of government, and to keep that division and distribution in effect for all time.

From their own pre-revolutionary experience, our forebears had learned that real liberty exists only where the power of government is strictly limited and where these limitations can be enforced directly by the very people over whom the power of government is exercised.

For our Revolutionary ancestors this was a self-evident truth about liberty, and it is reflected in every line of those constitutional limitations which they established to protect and preserve their freedom against the encroachments of their government.

Elsewhere in this book we have encountered Woodrow Wilson's warning against the consolidation of those powers which the Constitution distributed so widely through our complex of federal, state and local governments. Nevertheless, we have seen that such a consolidation has now taken place and has firmly congealed in Washington, D. C., with its hard center in the office of the President.

The existence of this great deposit of federal force makes a mockery of those carefully calculated checks, separations, balances and limitations which we still call the Constitution of the United States and which all federal officials from the President on down, each with a straight and solemn face, have sworn to uphold, observe and maintain.

Oaths to the contrary, our vaunted government of enforceable laws has long since disappeared into a huge maze of completely uncontrollable government by unpredictable men, most of whom are unknown to the great mass of the American people.

Nevertheless, all of these countless, nameless and powerful men are merely our servants and agents. In law, their authority to bind us who are their employers and their principals is restricted to narrow specified areas of official activity marked out in the Constitution, which is the agency contract between us and them and which is the sole basis of their authority to act for us.

Outside of those specified areas of authority, the legal effect of their actions upon us and upon our liberty and our property should be no more respectable and enforceable than the action of your real estate agent when he attempts to transfer the title, not to your real estate, but to your tractor, truck or automobile.

If your real estate agent did attempt to make such an un-authorized transfer, you could go into court and set the attempted unauthorized transfer aside. In the process you would recover your vehicle, together with compensation for any incidental damages to it or to you.

Why is it that we cannot do the same thing when our federal agents violate the letter and spirit of our agency contract, namely, the Constitution of the United States, which each and every one of them has sworn to uphold? The answer, as we documented it earlier, is that these Federal agents have immunized themselves from this natural, logical and legal form of retributive justice by the enactment of self-serving statutes, and an accumulation of deferential Court decisions which for all practical purposes leave the American citizen helpless to enforce the Constitution against its violation by governmental agents and governmental agencies.

Basic in this system of immunity for the federal agent in the course of its palpable violations of your personal rights is the ancient doctrine that "the king can do no wrong" and that, therefore, "His Majesty, the Sovereign" cannot be sued without his own consent. Of course, there is nothing in the Constitution about this, and superficial students of American history may have casually concluded that the American Revolution was a successful effort to bury all of these monarchial pretensions with the tea that Massachusetts patriots defiantly tossed into Boston Harbor. Nevertheless, the courts long ago resurrected this doctrine for the convenience of federal bureaucrats in their judicial tilts with their employers, namely, the American taxpayers. In so many words, all of this has been said before, but because of its importance to the efforts of the Conservative American to restore and keep his liberty it must be repeated and remembered, to wit: *In spite of your plainly created Constitutional right, you cannot assert that right affirmatively in court unless and until and to the extent merely that Congress has consented to let you do so.*[1]

Graciously, Congress has given its consent for your suit against the government in certain instances, but only with severe and special limitations and, if you think for a moment that you may proceed against the offending federal bureaucrat under the same procedural rules that govern your action against the offending real estate agent, then you have another think coming.

For instance, in your permissible suit against a federal agency for damages, the government has a complete defense if the act you complain about was performed by the federal agent in the exercise of his discretion, even though his judgment was notoriously bad.[2] Of course, your real estate agent could never get away with that kind of defense. And if the federal government takes your property for public use with compensation to you, which it has a constitutional right to do, of course, the proposed governmental use is "public" when the appropriate federal bureaucrat says it is, even though the only purpose of the "taking" is to get the private owner out of the neighborhood. The federal government is not required to submit itself to a public debate concerning its proposed use of the involved property. The amount of compensation is the only thing that the private property owner may contest in court, in spite of the fact that evidence is available to show that the proposed use is not public and/or that other land better suited to the proposed use is available at a more convenient location.[3] Can you think of any good reason why this evidence should be excluded and why the Court's jurisdiction should be restricted merely to the value of the condemned property? Such evi-

1 See Chapter 10, note 8, supra.
2 *Coates v. U.S.* 181 Fed. 2d 816, C.C.A. Mo. (1950).
3 *North Laramie Land Co. v. Hoffman,* 286 U.S. 276.

dence might slow down the process of making public property out of private property, but would that be bad?

The immunities which surround suits against the government itself likewise apply to the more than seven hundred tax-free business enterprises that the federal government operates in competition with private owners. These include loan agencies, TVA-type power companies, rope factories, and warehouses, among other things. The constitutional propriety of these private business operations is now beyond question in the courts. A mere taxpayer who pays the bill for the acquisition and operation of these tax-free competitions by the federal government with the taxpayers' own private taxpaying business, cannot bring a suit to test the constitutionality of this federal spending. The Supreme Court has said so,[4] and Congress, for all of its professed sensitivity on the subject of civil rights, has done nothing to enable the citizen to question its constitutional power to appropriate his money for anything and everybody all over the world.

The people and the organizations who are perpetually excited about the civil right of a person to refuse to salute the American flag, to refuse to take a loyalty oath as a condition for a federal scholarship, or to refuse to answer a Congressional inquiry into his subversive activities and/or associations, never say a word or lift a finger to re-establish the vanished right of a taxpayer to defend his wages and property affirmatively and/or defensively against the federal government in a federal court by the same historic processes of law that apply in similar suits by or against the butcher, the baker or the real estate agent.

When an ex-commissioner of Internal Revenue cried out far and wide against the police state methods that were and still are commonly used by federal income tax collectors[5]

---

[4] *Frothingham v. Mellon*, 262 U.S. 447, 1923.
[5] Chapter 12, note 20, supra.

against the people of the United States, his speeches brought no inquiries from the professional "bleeding hearts" who are perpetually fretful about the abuse of the rights of man, so-called.

Our pious oaths to support the Constitution of the United States are well and good, necessary and proper, but today they are a dime a dozen and are worth precisely that to the average American citizen whose constitutional rights against the government and particularly against the federal government are all but precluded from consideration by the courts. As they are being compiled now, federal court records reveal that you cannot get the protections of the Constitution in a formal legal action today, unless you are accused of a crime, suspected of Communism, or are fortunate enough to be a client of the National Association for the Advancement of Colored People. The success of the last named organization in establishing a new field of constitutional law that is readily and summarily enforceable, particularly in and by the Supreme Court of the United States, should be a lesson to disorganized citizens and taxpayers for whom the Constitution has become a dead letter. Perhaps the time has come for this big majority group to organize for the protection of its members in the courts.

"Civil rights," so called, are important but constitutional rights are even more important. A "civil right," as we have seen, is a privilege extended by some branch of the civil government. Among such privileges are the right to vote, to drive a car, to go to a public school, and, on the federal side, to get a passport or to go through bankruptcy. But constitutional rights are in a much higher category. President Kennedy said at his inauguration in 1961 that the Constitution protects "the rights of man" which come "not from the generosity of the State but from the hand of God." In this country a basic God-given right of every man is the right to enforce the Constitution against his government. That being so, neither Congress nor the courts, nor both together, should be able to create a Federal King who can do the very wrongs that the Constitution specifically prohibits, and escape responsibility for them. As the law now stands, taxpayers are second class citizens who are deprived of due process and equal protection of the laws. They must pay unequal taxes because their agent, the government, in violation of the contract of agency, decrees that they must do so and then shields itself from a legal attack upon this unauthorized act against its principal by a self-serving decree of immunity from suit. Taxpayers see their trustee (the federal government) violate the trust indenture (the Constitution) and dissipate the trust funds of the taxpayers by unauthorized indiscriminate donations to false friends and open enemies all over the world. For this notorious malfeasance, the trustor (the taxpayer) is left without a legal remedy by the trustee's own arbitrary decree.

The Conservative American believes that this sort of behavior makes a travesty of constitutional government. He finds no reference to "sovereignty" in the Constitution of the United States. He believes therefore that the doctrine of "sovereign immunity" is a parasitical growth upon our Constitutional system and that it should be cut out and discarded. He is convinced that the nature of constitutional government requires that the governmental agent shall be held to his constitutional contract the same as the real estate agent, and be liable to respond to the same kind of legal actions in the same kind of courts. He does not believe that our Constitution is lost. On the contrary, he is convinced that it is being deliberately concealed by public officials who are betraying their public trust. He wants to vote for candidates who will pledge themselves to bring the Constitution out of hiding and restore it to the government of the United States.

14

The Red Roadblock

☆☆☆☆☆

Shortly before he died (July 31, 1953) Senator Taft warned the Senate and the Eisenhower administration that none of the 1952 Republican campaign promises could be fulfilled unless and until our foreign policies were completely overhauled. In this valediction to his party and to the American people, Taft said that "the moral and political imperatives for a Senate audit of our foreign affairs from 1940 are beyond question. We cannot clean up the mess in Washington, balance the budget, reduce taxes, check creeping Socialism, tell what is muscle or fat in our sprawling re-armament programs or purge subversives from our State Department, unless we come to grips with our foreign policy upon which all other policies depend."

Since Taft said that, the weakness and ineptitude of the United States at home and abroad has worsened, at first steadily, then sharply and now, catastrophically. The reason for our declining strength and weakened purpose is the fact that Taft's dying declaration has been ignored.

Since the end of World War II, our foreign policy has been beleaguered by one—and only one—basic problem, namely, Communism. For twenty years we have been temporizing with the Communist menace instead of "coming to grips" with it as the first order of our moral and political duty. An elementary perception of the true nature of Communism clinches the conviction that we cannot co-exist with it for the same reason that we cannot co-exist with cholera, namely, that it is virulent, contagious and deadly. Official authorities on the disease called Communism, beginning with Karl Marx himself, have agreed that Communism will conquer everything that does not conquer Communism first, and the wide range of things that Communism is out to destroy certainly includes the United States of America.[1] From 1917 to 1933 four successive Presidents of the United States perceived and acknowledged the predatory, amoral nature of Communism and the characteristic criminality of Communist dictators. Each of these Presidents concluded that agreements and diplomatic contacts with Communist governments were, therefore, worse than useless.

In 1920, our government announced officially that the Communist regime in Russia was "based upon the negation of every principle of honor and good faith, and every usage and convention underlying the whole structure upon which it is possible to base harmonious and trustful relations whether of nations or of individuals." [2]

This official 1920 conclusion by the United States government was publicly confirmed in 1963 by Alexei Adzhubei, son-in-law of Kremlin Premier Nikita Khrushchev. Mr. Adz-

---

[1] The Committee on Un-American Activities of the House of Representatives has supervised the preparation of a series of volumes covering *Facts on Communism*. Volume 1, *The Communist Ideology* was authored by Dr. Gerhart Niemeyer, Professor of Political Science at the University of Notre Dame. This is a concise and accurate analysis of the true nature of Communism with full documentation. Those who are inclined to believe that conclusions about Communism found in *The Conservative American* are too categorical and/or sweeping should check them against Dr. Niemeyer's abundant documentation of *The Communist Ideology*. (Government Printing Office, No. 44836, 135 p., 45¢).

[2] See Statement of Secretary of State Colby quoted page 19, Chap. 2 infra.

hubei had just had a private audience with the late Pope John XXIII when newspapers asked the distinguished Communist emissary if he had discussed a possible agreement between the Kremlin and the Vatican. Mr. Adzhubei declared that no such agreement was contemplated because it would be useless. He was quoted by the reporters as follows:

"I am an atheist. I could break my word with the Holy Father. . . . As an atheist I would not be compelled to keep a promise. . . . There can never be peaceful co-existence between the Christian religion and our Communist doctrine." [3]

But in spite of our official discernment in 1920, frankly confirmed by Alexei Adzhubei forty-three years later, our government for thirty years has continued to negotiate agreements with the Kremlin which we have observed and which the Communists have broken at will. Since 1933, when President Roosevelt rescued the tottering Soviet regime with American recognition, the Communist contagion has infected the entire human race while its ravage has paralyzed the freedom of one billion people now held in Communist slavery. Millions of these victims are now in the western hemisphere and high up on the agenda of the relentless Communist conquest are the Panama Canal Zone and Puerto Rico. In spite of its perfidious record and the openly professed purposes and objectives of its authors and managers, our American foreign policy directorate stubbornly refuses to recognize that the Red conspiracy is a ruthless unmoral force that cannot rest until it has conquered everybody and everything on earth.

Our determination to avoid "coming to grips" with the reality of Communist criminality has now hardened into our

[3] Quoted by David Lawrence in *Buffalo (N.Y.) Evening News*, March 22, 1963.

present official policy which is to avoid a "confrontation" with the Communists at all hazards and to continue to pay them blackmail with our money and the liberty and territory of other people. Our government now stakes the future of mankind upon the official conviction that Communism is "mellowing" and that the behavior and purposes of Nikita Khrushchev are more malleable than those of his predecessors in the Red Kremlin hierarchy.[4] In the meantime, we concern ourselves officially lest rebellious slaves behind the Iron Curtain show less restraint than we do and take matters into their own hands as in Hungary in 1956. *The New York Times,* always a reliable guide through the thicket of our international "bi-partisan" foreign policy, put it this way:

[4] "As long as capitalism and socialism exist, we cannot live in peace. In the end, one or the other will triumph. A funeral dirge will be sung either over the Soviet Republic or over world capitalism." Speech delivered by Lenin, November 26, 1920. *Selected Works,* (International Publishers, New York, 1943), Vol. VIII, p. 297.

"The victory of Communism is historically inevitable. . . . We are confidently going along our direct road which was pointed out by Marx, Engels, and Lenin." Khrushchev speech of June 2, 1956, quoted by *Soviet Affairs,* Notes. October 14, 1957. No. 215, p. 2.

The House of Representatives Committee on Un-American Activities has compiled and published seven volumes (approximately 4500 pages) of sworn testimony describing "The Crimes of Khrushchev." The synopsis of Volume 1 begins: "Khrushchev, as the No. 1 Communist official in the Moscow area, sent thousands to their death, scores of thousands to hideous slave labor camps. He was sent in 1937, as Stalin's trusted killer, to the Ukraine. . . . When his two year Ukranian purge was over, an estimated 400,000 had been killed and terror gripped the whole population."

The testimony of these witnesses was being taken while Khrushchev was President Eisenhower's official guest at the White House and at Camp David in 1959.

See Willard Edwards, *Manion Forum Broadcast 420,* October 14, 1962, also *"The Fringe on Top"* (p. 142 et seq) by Stanton Evans et al, American Features, New York.

"We must seek to discourage anti-Communist revolts in order to avert bloodshed and war. We must *under our principles* (sic) live with evil even if by doing so we help to stabilize tottering Communist regimes, as in East Germany, and perhaps even expose citadels of freedom, like West Berlin, to slow death by strangulation." [5]

The Conservative American cannot fathom the motivation of an American foreign policy that gives our official protection to the boundaries of Communist slavery (as in Cuba, East Germany and Hungary) but permits Communist invasion of the free world at any point at any time (as in South Vietnam, Tibet, Venezuela and British Guiana).

At the moment of this writing we are sending American soldiers ten thousand miles to fight Communists in South Vietnam while we are arresting Americans and Cuban exiles who attempt to fight the Communists in Cuba which is only ninety miles from che coast of Florida. In this process of continuous retreat we boast of preserving "peace" which is precisely what the Kremlin calls its eminently successful tactic of "liberating" one free world country after another into Communist captivity by means of riots, subversion and mob violence, stimulated and supervised by its ubiquitous resident agents. Our State Department envisions a long protraction of this "peaceful competition" between our "open society" and the "closed society" called Communism. In what they plan to be our completely disarmed world of the future our diplomats see no reason why this competition should not go on indefinitely until the two rival systems are merged into some sort of political and economic consensus.

In the plain everyday language of the Conservative American, what our State Department is proposing is the abject surrender of our freedom and national independence. Fortunately, there is available to Congress and to the American

[5] August 16, 1961.

people a scientific and thoroughly effective antidote for this poisonous policy.

Continuously, for forty years our government has retained the full-time services of an internationally renowned specialist on the subject of Communism. The advice he gives, upon request, to government officials is a classified secret but periodically J. Edgar Hoover makes public statements in the course of which he reiterates the substance of what he said to the National Convention of the American Legion at Las Vegas, Nevada, in October, 1962:

"We are at war with this sinister conspiracy [Communism]. Every Communist today must be considered our enemy wherever he may be, at home or abroad. A 'soft' approach toward the menace of Communism can lead only to national disaster."

In the same address Mr. Hoover said:

"Today there are 925 Soviet and satellite official personnel in the United States. The vast majority of them constitute a cunning and dangerous espionage threat. From the immunity of their diplomatic assignments, representatives of Communist-bloc nations have directed intelligence networks within the United States.

"From 1950 through 1960, 21 officials of the Soviet Union alone were declared persona non grata, or otherwise asked to leave the country. One Soviet defector, a former intelligence official, has estimated that between 70 and 80 per cent of the Soviet officials in the United States have espionage assignments.

"Duplicity and deceit are inherent in every phase of the international Communist conspiracy. During the last 30 years the United States has participated in hundreds of meetings with the Communists—Teheran, Yalta, Potsdam, Panmunjon and Geneva. These meetings led to many agreements, almost all of which have been broken by Soviet Russia."

Mr. Robert Kennedy, as Attorney General of the United States, called Mr. Hoover "my professional" on the subject of Communism. Mr. Hoover is indeed the "professional" of and for the entire United States government on that critical subject. That being so, the Conservative American wonders why the State Department has ignored Mr. Hoover's professional findings and listened instead to Dr. Walt Rostow, who has no obvious background of experience with the Communist conspiracy, and, who, for that reason, perhaps, has maintained that "peace" and a "consensus" is on the agenda of Soviet-American relationships.

If a private citizen were caught dealing with a Communist agent, Mr. Hoover, as Director of the F.B.I., would put such citizen under continuous surveillance. How is this proper precautionary practice reconciled with our continuous, open and secret deals with the enemy at the top diplomatic levels? If, as Mr. Hoover submits, "between 70 and 80 per cent of the Soviet officials in the United States have espionage assignments," then the odds are either 7 to 3 or 8 to 2 that the Soviet diplomats who are talking to our representatives in Washington and/or at the United Nations about our disarmament and other things are Communist spies. Are the "agreements" that come out of these conferences to be accepted at face value and are we prepared to liquidate our national defenses as a result of these negotiations?

The Conservative American would like to have Mr. J. Edgar Hoover answer these questions before the United States Senate Committee on Foreign Relations and before the Senate Armed Services Committee. The Conservative American is convinced that Mr. Hoover is correct. We *are* at war with Communism. This war is the inevitable and unceasing conflict between two squarely and flatly contradictory institutions, namely, Americanism and Communism. Communism is by its profession, nature, practice and purpose an unequivocal denial of every one of the four basic supporting affirmations of Americanism.

The first basic American affirmation is the existence, power and providence of Almighty God. We made this affirmation with the first breath of the new life of our Republic. In the American Declaration of Independence we proclaimed that the existence of God is a self-evident truth. We said that God exists: not as a matter of faith but as a matter of fact. This truth is the basic first cornerstone of our politically organized society. Without God, none of our legal and political institutions makes sense.

Communism hits this affirmation "head-on." Communism is the activation of militant marching atheism. Every single one of its plans, purposes and postulates is predicated upon the assumption that the only acceptable omnipotence is the ruling Communist dictatorship. The slightest compromise with this assumption would cause the whole Communist apparatus to fall apart.

The second basic American affirmation is the temporal and eternal *personal* responsibility of the individual citizen. As Madison stated in the *Federalist*,[6] our entire political experiment swings upon our capacity to govern ourselves according to the moral law. It was upon this assumption that the Founding Fathers moved on to the third supporting pillar of our system, namely, constitutionally limited government. The only people who can afford the great luxury of a civil government strictly limited by law are those people who recognize and are willing to live by their natural, God-imposed obligations and responsibilities under the Ten Commandments. In the Pennsylvania wilderness, a hundred years before Madison was born, William Penn had declared that "those people who will not be governed by God will be ruled by tyrants." The prescient leaders, who with Madison,

6 Number 39.

put the great timbers of our Constitutional structure in place, remembered that, too. There is no protection against tyranny nor for the endurance and conservation of constitutional limitation upon the power of government, except in the moral government of each man by his faith and by himself, under God.

The activated atheism called Communism sweeps away both of these American affirmations at the same time: In the Communist dispensation there are no God-given rights and no God-imposed responsibilities because there is no God but the State. Under Communism, human beings are merely in the higher order of material "things." Under such circumstances, constitutional limitations would be an insult to the ruling authorities who are the absolute owners and commanders of every person and thing under their jurisdiction.

The final basic affirmation of Americanism is the natural institution of private property which it is the primary purpose of Communism to destroy.[7]

At every pivotal point, therefore, sparks fly and shocks reverberate when Communism confronts Americanism. The Communists have never hesitated to proclaim this generic incompatibility of their institution with ours, and the refusal of our foreign policy governors to recognize it now as clearly as they did in 1920 is inexplicable.[8]

The Conservative American wants this state of war, which has been acknowledged by J. Edgar Hoover, to be declared and acknowledged by the Congress of United States. Resolutions have been introduced in Congress to bring about such a declaration and the Conservative American believes that

[7] See Chapter 12.

[8] "We must recognize that we cannot co-exist eternally, for a long time. We do not want to go to the grave. They [meaning the Americans] do not want to go to their grave, either. So what can be done? *We must push them to their grave.*"

(Public statement by Khrushchev in Warsaw, Poland, April, 1955.)

these should be revived and supported.[9] We cannot go forward with the restoration and conservation of our basic American resources, namely, personal liberty, constitutional government and national independence until the big Red roadblock is removed from the pathway of human freedom here and all over the world.

The Communists have blackmailed the whole course of their brutal conquest across the world with the threat of nuclear war. This criminal operation, like all successful blackmail, has been predicated upon the calculated weakness of the victim rather than the strength of the criminal who has practiced it. The victim of highway robbery may lose his money but he can keep his self-respect. The victim of blackmail loses both, not once merely but time and again interminably.

Because Stalin threatened to make a separate peace with Hitler, we gave him his "second front" in France rather than through the "soft underbelly" at the Balkans which would have shut him off from his coveted conquest of Eastern Europe. When Stalin threatened to destroy President Roosevelt's dream of the United Nations, we forgot the matter of free elections and gave him a free hand with one hundred million formerly free people in more than twenty previously independent nations. Because Khrushchev threatened nuclear war, we permitted him to build the Berlin Wall and promised to protect from invasion his new Communist colony in the Western Hemisphere.[10]

[9] Congressman John R. Pillion (*New York Manion Forum broadcast 359*, August 13, 1961.)

[10] "In what way have we retreated, one may ask. Socialist Cuba exists, Cuba remains a beacon of Marxist, Leninist ideas in the Western Hemisphere. The impact of her (Cuba's) revolutionary example will grow. The government of the United States has given a pledge not to invade Cuba. The threat of thermonuclear war has been averted. Is this a retreat?"

(Nikita Khrushchev in a public statement on December 13, 1962.)

In the passionate pursuit of "peace" we now propose to disarm ourselves and hand over the problem of our national defense to the tender mercies of the United Nations while we engage in "trade" with our implacable Communist enemies.

Criminologists recognize that the victim of blackmail has three and only three possible courses of action against his criminal tormentor. The victim may (a) continue to pay the blackmailer, or (b) he may kill the blackmailer, or (c) he may free himself by telling the truth that he is paying the blackmailer to conceal.

For twenty years our government has been paying the Soviet blackmailer with one concession after another. It is obvious now that the extortioner will be satisfied with nothing short of the complete and unconditional surrender of our national life. To "kill" the blackmailer might or might not require a nuclear war but for those who would "rather be Red than dead," there is still the third alternative: *We can tell the truth* and the truth—now as in 1776—will make us free.

The truth is that there is no such thing as a *legitimate* Communist government anywhere on earth. The truth is that what our State Department calls the "closed societies" of Communism are iron-ringed jails from which the inmates may attempt to escape only at the risk of their lives. The truth is that conditions in these Communist jails are so horrible that hundreds of people risk and often lose their lives in attempts to escape from them. The truth is that the hundreds of millions of helpless people who are held in this monstrous Red captivity are scandalized by the calloused indifference of our government to their cruel fate as expressed in a foreign policy which is deliberately calculated to "help stabilize tottering Communist regimes, as in East Germany."

The truth is that without our positive and active help, all

of these "tottering Communist regimes" would fall of their own weight within six months after our help was withdrawn.

The truth is that if we withdrew our official prohibition against an invasion of the Red Chinese mainland by the Nationalist Chinese Army on Formosa that invasion would take place immediately, and 90 per cent of the enslaved Chinese on the mainland would join the attack against their Red Chinese jailers.

This would solve our problem in South Vietnam and Laos where the Red forces are being supplied and supervised by the Red Chinese government. The collapse of Communism in China would start a chain reaction of anti-Communist revolution which would sweep across Europe to the eastern boundary of West Germany.

The consequences of *an official proclamation of the truth about Communists and Communist governments by the government of the United States* would open the door to the destruction of Communism by its own oppressed victims without international war and without the use of American military forces.

The truth is that we are deliberately helping the Communist dictators to remain in power because the liberal-internationalist establishment which has controlled our government for thirty years wishes to use Communism as a ploy to bring about the eventual establishment of a "consensus," namely universal "Democratic-Socialism" under World Government.

The Conservative American knows that the cry of "peace, peace, when there is no peace" but only continuous surrender to a relentless foe in a world-wide war is sheer political hypocrisy. He realizes that little or nothing can be done about the conservation of our eroding resources of precious moral principle until we "come to grips" with Communism which is now reversing the course of western civilization and turning it into a torrent of atheistic barbarism.

The truth that made us free will restore our freedom now and lift the hearts and hopes of millions whom our present policy of retreat and surrender has doomed to perpetual slavery. Let us therefore tell the truth. The Conservative American believes that:

"We should declare the world Communist movement an outlaw in the community of civilized nations. Accordingly, we should withdraw diplomatic recognition from all Communist governments, including that of the Soviet Union, thereby serving notice on the world that we regard such governments as neither legitimate nor permanent." [11]

This will not be a signal for international nuclear war but for successful anti-Communist revolution which will melt down the Iron Curtain from the inside. This is the high road of moral principle that leads to peace with freedom for America and for mankind.

[11] *The Conscience of A Conservative*, by Barry Goldwater, (Victor Publishing Company, Shepardsville, Kentucky, 1960) p. 120.

Index

☆☆☆☆☆